What The Holy Spirit Taught Me This Morning

A Devotional with a Difference

Amos Dele Dada PhD; P. Eng (Chem Eng); DPC
International Gathering of Eagles Series.

authorHOUSE®

AuthorHouse™
1663 Liberty Drive
Bloomington, IN 47403
www.authorhouse.com
Phone: 1 (800) 839-8640

For further information, contact :
Pastor Amos Dada
amos.dada@gmail.com
Tel: +1(416)6162425
www.cacbethel.com
www.igoeministry.com
22-94 Kenhar Dr Toronto
ON M9L 1N2
Canada

Published by AuthorHouse 09/07/2018

ISBN: 978-1-5462-3528-6 (sc)
ISBN: 978-1-5462-3527-9 (e)

Library of Congress Control Number: 2018903805

Print information available on the last page.

Contents

Dedication

This book is lovingly dedicated to my daughters and granddaughters
Oluwadara Ayoola
Oluwatoyin Crandell
Ifeolouwa Dada
Oluwatobi Dada
Deborah Dada
Josephine Verniege
Maranatha Crandell
Iyanuoluwa Ayoola

Many daughters have done virtuously but thou excellest them all
–Proverbs 31:29 KJV

This book is graciously dedicated to all that will be inspired by it. Those who will diligently observe their morning quiet time and use it as a time to listen to the still small voice of God and go ahead and win the battles of life but more importantly affect their generation positively! Are you that person?

This book is humbly dedicated to Elder Samuel Oluwabusuyi Dada A.K.A Jesulakoyosayemi (of blessed memory) and Deaconess Victoria Aduola Dada, my lovely parents for inculcating in me the art of observing morning devotion in my early years.

Acknowledgement

This book would not be born if I was not born. I want to acknowledge my loving parents Elder Samuel Oluwabusuyi Dada (A.K.A Jesuslakoyosayemi) and Deacon Victoria Adunola Dada (A.K.A Eyekoyosi) for bringing me forth physically and spiritually. More importantly for training me to observe my quiet time by practical example. My father was the one who rang the bell for morning devotion at Christ Apostolic Church Oke-Igbala Odoigede and later Christ Apostolic Church Oke-Ayo in Igede-Ekiti. In between the ringing of the first and second bell he would faithfully wake us up to have morning devotion as a family between 4:30am and 5am. Then, we would all go to church from 5am to 6am for general church morning devotion. It was very difficult to wake up in those days but it has paid off now. I am grateful. Also to my wife- Lady Evangelist Fyitayo Folashade Dada and children: Oluwadara Temitope Ayoola, Oluwatoyin Ayodeji Crandell, Ifeolouwa Oluwasaanumi Dada, Oluwatobi Victoria Dada, Deborah Ayomide Dada who endured me also when following my parents footstep and I insisted they too must observe morning devotion even in Canada. Though most times they were half awake and half asleep!

I also want to acknowledge all my contacts on WhatsApp and Facebook who were blessed by these weekly postings and encouraged me to put it into a book. To members of our great church, Christ Apostolic Church Bethel Toronto, (the church where the Lord answers prayers) who gave me the platform to share these messages with them, I want to say thank you.

I want to acknowledge, my guitarist who also became my proof reader, Spencer Reid, for a great job and Deborah Dada who designed the cover page. Also worthy of acknowledgment is Deborah Zikos who selected the images.

I want to acknowledge The General Superintendent of Christ Apostolic Church World Wide, Pastor S.O.A Oladele, one of the most erudite teachers of our time, for taking the time out of his very busy schedule to write the foreword for this book. I am grateful.

Finally to all that are too numerous to mention that contributed to the success of printing this book, God bless you in Jesus' name.

Foreword

"A new heart also will I give you, and a new spirit will I put within you: and I will take away the stony heart out of your flesh, and I will give you an heart of flesh." Eze. 36: 26.

There is something frightening about stones as used by Prophet Ezekiel in the above metaphor. Stones are hard, weather-beaten and impervious to the most comforting liquid. They lack all the attributes of living things. No mobility, no growth, no respiration, no reproduction and no response to stimuli. They are dead.

A heart in this condition is useless to humanity and that heart can never be useful to God either. It is the heart of sin. It is the heart depicting spiritual blindness, deafness and dumbness. The heart that sees nothing and can hear nothing. It is a heart which has shut itself against the Word and invariably against the world.

But there is divine intervention in that same verse 26: "and I will give you an heart of flesh". There is further affirmation of this in verse 27: "and I will put my spirit within you, and cause you to walk in my statutes, and ye shall keep my judgments and do them".

Here lies the problem of Christianity today; while God is still willing to give people this heart of flesh and He is still anxious to put His spirit within His people so that they may walk in His statutes, unfortunately, many are too busy to give what it takes to receive these free gifts of God. This can be seen in some people's lack of real prayer life. Many still don't have the time to study His word in order to hear from Him.

Prophet Isaiah wrote: "…in returning and rest shall ye be saved, in quietness and in confidence shall be your strength…" Isa. 30: 15. It follows therefore that a Christian can't walk with God, neither can he grow in the spirit without having an intimate relationship with God in His Word and without talking to Him in prayers.

For many who want to have that relationship with God but have no idea how to go about it, Pastor AMOS DELE DADA has come to their rescue with this book: "WHAT THE HOLY SPIRIT TAUGHT ME THIS MORNING". This is a collection of the record of his quiet time with God. The subjects discussed vary and each subject provides impactful spiritual insights into numerous issues of life.

He has provided a compass for many to navigate their ways on the ocean of life. I have read excerpts from the book and I am satisfied with the sheer orthodoxy of his teaching and the masterful articulation of his points. I have no doubt that this book will enrich Christian devotions. I, therefore, recommend it to every believer willing to grow in the spirit.

PASTOR SAMUEL O. OLADELE
General Superintendent, Christ Apostolic Church

Preface

Any time I am doing my quiet time, I hear God teaching me and giving me deep revelations in the scripture. I believe they are very profound, revealing, informative, educative and highly inspiring. For several years, I just prayed on them and at times used some of the notes for my weekly sermons; however, with the advent of social media, I discovered that I could share such messages with others. When I did the response was very encouraging.

Though I post it weekly on my Facebook and WhatsApp, I discovered I was still limited. Hence, I took it to my blog and with the encouragement of relations, colleagues and church family, it has metamorphosed to a book!

My intention in writing this book is to encourage you to do your quiet time. This is the time God uses to teach you something special from the scriptures; that can benefit you and others when making your daily decisions. So, make it a daily practice to leave all books behind. Just read the Bible and listen to what God has to say to you and share it with humanity. This devotional is not a replacement for your bible it is a supplement.

The content of these revelations have high spiritual voltage, that I am sure will bless you. More than that, it will inspire you to find your purpose, be earthly relevant and heavenly conscious. Moreover, it will enable you find meaning for your life, living a life of integrity and soaring as an eagle in your spiritual, physical, academic, matrimonial and financial positioning.

Amos Dele Dada
May 2018

1

Where Are You Going: Nineveh Or Tarshish?

"1. Arise, go to Nineveh, that great city, and cry against it; for their wickedness is come up before me. 3. But Jonah rose up to flee to Tarshish......" Jonah 1:2,3 [KJV]

- ◆ Where are you going? Nineveh or Tarshish?
- ◆ Where are you going this year?
- ◆ Where are you rushing to with your bag and baggage?
- ◆ Where is your career going?
- ◆ Where is your marriage going?
- ◆ Where is your spinsterhood heading to?
- ◆ Where are you going as a bachelor?
- ◆ Where is your ministry going?
- ◆ Where are you going as a Pastor, Evangelist, Bishop, General Overseer, Apostle where?
- ◆ Where are you going as a father, mother, husband, wife, where?

Young man, young woman, where are you going academically? Nineveh or, Tarshish? God's destination or yours?

You determined where you are going despite God's good plan for you. You claim you are born again. Very good. God acknowledges it. God now tells you, 'now that you are born again arise for the salvation of others.'

'Now that you have a job go and assist someone else.' 'Now that you are anointed, minister peace and healing to someone else.'

God now sends you to Nineveh. Where have you decided to go?

See, Jonah rose up to flee to Tarshish. Why are you going to Tarshish instead of Nineveh? Belly of the fish for you!

Just imagine the scene when Jonah was buying a ticket from Joppa to Tarshish. Why are you spending the money, talent, treasures and time God gave you, to work against Him?

"But the Lord sent a great wind…" Jonah 1:4 Why not!?

God is still sending troubles, storms, unpleasant circumstances to disobedient children. "Maybe it is not Satan, that put you in this unpleasant situation, maybe you provoked God to 'create' it for you." My counsel from today; simply obey God.

> "Maybe it is not Satan, that put you in this unpleasant situation, maybe you provoked God to 'create' it for you."

Tarshish means 'greedy one', Nineveh means 'propagate', 'increase'. In sending Jonah to Nineveh, God wanted to kill two birds with one stone. Prosper Jonah and save Nineveh; but, Jonah went to Tarshish pursuing greed. Stop pursuing greed. Stop destroying yourself!

God is sending you to a Nineveh this year. Save yourself from great storms of life and ending in the belly of a fish; just go! More importantly, there are souls, waiting for you to just 'speak the Word' and they shall repent and be saved. In your office, neighbourhood, and school, wherever you find yourself 'speak the Word'. Guess what, after going through all the trouble you will still go to Nineveh, by force, and by fire! So, why don't you just obey now? It is called TQM (Total Quality Management). Doing it right the first time. They used to tell us in the Yoruba language in those days in Sunday School, "Egberun Samuel ko le sa mo 'Olorun lowo," that is: a thousand Samuels cannot run away from God successfully. You cannot run away from God successfully. He is a sovereign God!

He does whatsoever pleases him- Psalm 115:3!

Go to Nineveh now!

Prayer : O Lord, help me to learn obedience from Jonah. Let me not enter the belly of a fish, that is, put myself in a terrible situation before I do your will.

Quotation: *"Now if you obey me fully and keep my covenant, then out of all nations you will be my treasured possession. Although the whole earth is mine,"* - **God Almighty** (Exodus 19: 5)

> *Obedience brings peace in decision making. If we have firmly made up our minds to follow the commandments, we will not have to redecide which path to take when temptation comes our way.* **-James E. Faust**

2

Strategies To Turn Your Adversity Into Prosperity: Wagons Are Coming!

"Then Pharaoh said to Joseph, "Tell your brothers, 'Take wagons from the land of Egypt to carry your little children and your wives and bring your father here. 20 Don't worry about your personal belongings, for the best of all the land of Egypt is yours. 21 So the sons of Jacob did as they were told. Joseph provided them with wagons, as Pharaoh had commanded, and he gave them supplies for the journey. 22 And he gave each of them new clothes—but to Benjamin, he gave five changes of clothes and 300 pieces of silver. 23 He also sent his father ten male donkeys loaded with the finest products of Egypt, and ten female donkeys loaded with grain and bread and other supplies he would need on his journey." - Genesis 45:17-22

Above is the authoritative declaration of Pharaoh-the most powerful man and monarch at that time-to Joseph concerning his father, Jacob and his brothers. You know the story too well for me to bother you with details, but this is what Gen 45 teaches us: you cannot kill

> "If God has blessed a man, you are wasting your time trying to destroy him. Your act of wickedness will only catapult him to greater greatness."

another man's dream. Instead of wasting your time trying to kill another man's dream, spend that energy building your own dream. "If God has blessed a man, you are wasting your time trying to destroy him. Your act of wickedness will only catapult him to greater greatness." No amount of wickedness man is doing to you will stand. Focus on your dream, exercise your talents, do your due diligence (work), stand upon the pedestal of integrity, accountability and transparency to God and to man. Avoid touching the three 'Gs': The Gold, The Girls, and The Glory. Forgive those who have offended you, they are agents to lead you to a glorious destiny. That child they told you is dead, is alive, ignore the blood soaked coat of many colours. Have faith in the God that spoke to you. Gen. 28. Know this, man can only take away what man has given, not what God has deposited in you. You will rise again! Your day of receiving wagons is here today and ahead of you!

I prophesy to you this year, as Jacob received wagons from Pharaoh through Joseph, you will receive wagons from God Almighty:

- ◆ Wagons of a good spouse.
- ◆ Wagons of childbearing.
- ◆ Wagons of silver, gold, money- money is a defense. Eccl 7:12
- ◆ Wagons of joy.
- ◆ Wagons of promotion.
- ◆ Wagons of academic success.
- ◆ Wagons of men and women of integrity are coming to be part of your ministry.

- ◆ Wagons of the special blessings you need. Psalm 37:4
- ◆ Wagons of staff of substance are coming to join your business.
- ◆ Wagons of customers, clients, contracts, church members are coming.
- ◆ Wagons of material, spiritual, physical, matrimonial, financial blessing!

> You will have supplies for your journey. Say it loud! My wagons of blessing are coming!

Joseph singled out Benjamin, someone will single you out for a special blessing. As you witness for the Lord, and testify of His goodness and go out for evangelism to win souls, and preach the gospel of Jesus Christ; wagons, male donkeys (SUVs, trucks, etc.) and female donkeys (saloon cars) shall bring blessings to you.

They thought you were dead, but you are the anointed one to position your family to greatness.

What wagons are you believing God for? Vocalize it now, to the God that answers prayers! In your year of prosperity, you will receive your wagons in Jesus name. Jesus is Lord!

Prayer: O' Lord, let my wagons come and come speedily, (mention your needs now to the God of heaven and earth).

Quotation: "Don't block your blessings. Don't let doubt stop you from getting where you want to be." **-Jennifer Hudson**

3

The God That I serve

"Very early the next morning, the king got up and hurried out to the lions' den. 20 When he got there, he called out in anguish, "Daniel, servant of the living God! Was your God, whom you serve so faithfully, able to rescue you from the lions?"21 Daniel answered, "Long live the king! 22 My God sent his angel to shut the lions' mouths so that they would not hurt me, for I have been found innocent in his sight. And I have not wronged you, Your Majesty." - Daniel 6:20 NLT

Daniel proved that the key to a miracle is believing and serving God faithfully.

Notice the question from King Darius, the God that you serve so faithfully...

Do you serve God faithfully, or shabbily, nonchalantly, insolently, carelessly or indolently? **"The way you serve God will determine the way he will respond to you in the day of adversity."** You say, Pastor, God loves me unconditionally, that is true, as he loves every other person. But, the way you serve God will distinguish you from other people and determine the way he will respond in the day of adversity. If you care to know, God loved those who plotted Daniel's tragedy unconditionally; but they refused to serve God and the Lions did not spare them as they spared Daniel.

But the beauty of today's scripture is, that when you serve God faithfully you can make these demands and confess:

- The God that I serve will prosper me. The God that I serve will deliver me.
- The God that I serve will bless me. The God that I serve will save me.
- The God that I serve will protect me. The God that I serve will revive me.
- The God that I serve will provide for me. The God that I serve will make a difference in my life
- The God that I serve will not allow me to suffer deportation.
- The God that I serve will not allow me to be barren.
- The God that I serve will give me wisdom, knowledge and understanding.
- The God that I serve will help my ministry.
- The God that I serve will help me, academically, spiritually, materially, physically, financially, matrimonially.
- The God that I serve will not allow me to die in the den of lions and lionesses.
- The God that I serve will not allow my ministry, calling and destiny to be aborted.
- The God that I serve will empower me.
- The God that I serve will not allow me to be barren physically and mentally.
- The God that I serve will energize me in the place of prayer.
- The God that I serve will help me to study the word and live by the word.
- The God that I serve will make me a blessing to my generation.
- The God that I serve will help me to train my children and grandchildren in the way of God.
- The God that I serve will help me to do exploits for God. Daniel 11:32
- The God that I serve will not allow me to be sick or sickly.
- The God that I serve will saturate my ministry with miracles, signs, and wonders.
- The God that I serve will not allow me to suffer, shame and disgrace in the hand of my enemies.

- The God that I serve will bless me and make me a blessing to this generation.
- The God that I serve will showcase me for his glory.
- The God that I serve will bring me out of prison, sickness, depression, frustration, limitation, bondages, calamities, catastrophes, debt, whoredom, addiction, perversion, fornication, adultery, alcoholism, suicidal thoughts, evil company, disgrace...
- The God that I serve will deliver me from joblessness, bachelorhood, spinsterhood, troubled marriage.
- The God that I serve will empower me with the Holy Ghost.
- The God that I serve will help me to be wise enough to win souls.
- The God that I serve will help me to become a world changer.
- The God that I serve will keep me holy and help me to live a life of dignity not impunity, integrity not corruption or, evil.

I prophesy to you, the God you serve will honour your prayer in Jesus name.

Prayer: O' Lord, the God that I serve, come to my aid, as you did for Daniel in the time of adversity.

Quotation: "The best way to not feel hopeless is to get up and do something. Don't wait for good things to happen to you. If you go out and make some good things happen, you will fill the world with hope, you will fill yourself with hope." — **Barack Obama**

4

Life Will Not Be Difficult For You! (Part 1)

"They shall not be ashamed in the evil time: and in the days of famine they shall be satisfied." Psalm 37:19 [KJV]

Do you believe in prophecy? Do you believe in the word of God? Do you believe in God's providence, principles and promises? God is not a casual talker. God is not an uncalculated personality; he speaks with precision.

One of my relations called me last week: "things are so hard in Nigeria, please send any money you can afford to send. We are starving." Sometime ago I was in London, England where I had accommodation in a couple of places. As I woke up in one of the places, my hostess came and said, I should read a text from one of her acquaintances in Nigeria. It read: 'I beg you my wife and I and my children need food. Send money to us nothing is too small and nothing is too big'.

This is the reality in most developing countries. Using the Nigerian example, on Facebook, you will see a comparison of food prices tomatoes, rice, palm oil and yam showing exponential escalation, not just increases. I read on the Internet last month, about a pastor in Akure saying, 'there is no money in church because the salaries of workers have not been paid.' Citizens in many states in the nation are not being paid salaries. One governor even challenged his people, saying: 'do you want me to sell my wife and children to pay you?'

All these and more could be summarized in one word "famine." There is famine, not only in Nigeria. The times are hard. If you like, blame past or present governments, it doesn't change the reality. You can even blame global crash of crude oil prices. There is famine everywhere!

Then I read the scripture above- in the 'time of famine I shall be satisfied.' Psalm 37:19. Since the word of God must not go unfulfilled the question you must be asking is, how?

How do you get satisfied in the time of famine? How do you have surplus in the time of famine? Let me proffer three broad principles and solutions:

♦ **Sow**   ♦ **Expect Divine Supply**   ♦ **Engage In Prayer**

PART A. *Sow:*

The time of famine is a time of opportunity. It is a time of innovation and creativity. It is a time to work hard, as well as one to think through and rethink. It is a time to sow.

In Genesis 26:12-13, the Bible says Isaac sowed in the land and he prospered. I know I will step on toes now with my pastors, fathers in the Lord and colleagues who have always attributed 'sowing' here to giving an offering. Is that what the Bible says? What is sowing? Sowing is planting, farming, working and harvesting. It has not changed.

There was so much opposition and famine in the land, a lot of 'herdsmen' (Philistines) blocking Abraham's wells. That represents the previous economy. But Isaac devised means, worked very hard, persevered and prospered in the time of famine.

> "With the divine, massive arable land God has given Nigeria-cultivatable all year round, why should we languish in famine!?"

I hear God calling all nations, but, let me use Nigerians, both at home and in the diaspora, as an example; seize this moment to rethink. Till the ground! Just as God commanded Adam. "With the divine, massive arable land God has given Nigeria-cultivatable all year round, why should we languish in famine!?" Not even to talk of the amazingly talented human potential in the nation. I challenge the federal, state and municipal governments; churches, families and individuals to seize this moment, to go beyond Bible study. Jump to Bible application and change our nations!

Last year I was in Malaysia, and you need to see how a nation is prospering on Palm oil plantations.

As a man thinks, so is he. We must stop looking at this or that president or political candidate as our God. We must stop looking at governors as our God. They are not God! They have responsibilities they must not shy away from. This message is for them, as well as for individuals. The economic problems have gotten so bad that youth can no longer afford to wait for white collar jobs anymore. White, blue, black, red, there just aren't any jobs available! Now is the time to be proactive and go make job opportunities! This is the moment for Nigeria to arise and prosper. This is the moment to stop sending texts abroad looking for relations to send money. Your blessings are not to come from 'abroad' but from 'above'.

This is the time to sow- go to the 'farm' practically. Start that business you have procrastinated about, team up with peers and creatively develop the nation's economy.

Robert Schuller has these two quotations that resonate with me:

"Tough times never last but tough people do!" and "Always look at what you have left; never look at what you have lost."

It is time to take God by His words 'in the time of famine you shall be satisfied.' The question we should ask and solve is: how?

This is part one of the three ways the Holy Spirit put in my heart this morning.

It is time for you to be satisfied in the time of famine. It is our month of victory. We shall overcome if we choose to!

Prayer: Teach me Oh Lord to work hard in the time of famine. To sow my intelligence, talent and creative abilities.

Quotation: *"A dream doesn't become reality through magic; it takes sweat, determination and hard work."* **-Colin Powell**

5

Life Will Not Be Difficult
For You (Part 2)

PART B. *Expect Divine Supply*

> *"They shall not be ashamed in the evil time: and in the days of famine they shall be satisfied."* Psalm 37:19 [KJV]

Knowing fully well the word of God will come to pass universally, you must personally choose to be a partaker in this phrase "'in the time of famine we shall be satisfied.'" This is premised on the fact that right now, globally, everybody is screaming famine, both the led and the leaders.

Whereas, in the first write up I expressed the practical steps to take: **Sow**! Now, I want to focus on the spiritual: **Divine Supply**.

In the time of famine you shall be satisfied means, there will be "divine supply". God will use his sovereignty combined with his nature of love, kindness, and mercy to ensure that your needs are supernaturally met.

Our God is the Master of the game of "Divine Supply." In the Bible, we find seven classic cases:

♦ Elijah in the wilderness	1 King 17:6	♦ Samaria in time of famine	2 Kings 7:8
♦ The army of the three kings	2 King 3:20	♦ The multitude that followed Christ	Matt 14:20
♦ The prophets widow	2 Kings 4:6	♦ The Saints	Phil 4:19
♦ People of Israel (Manna)	Ex 16:13-15		

There are factors that make God pull out resources from his divine warehouse to his people. Those factors are covenant relationships and faith. That is, trust in The Lord. Here the question is, do we have a covenant relationship with God like that of Israel? Yes! Scattered all over the nations are strong believers. If we follow the account in Genesis 18:32, God and Abraham's encounter concerning Sodom and Gomorrah; if God will find ten righteous people in the land it will be saved. Is the question here more according to the remnant of faith? I am sure it is.

I am sure, if you connect to this covenant something will happen. In a few months there will be a supernatural turnaround. Somebody replied to part one saying that Nigeria needs rain. I have good news for you. Within the ambits and purview of divine supply, God will send rain. Meaning physical rain, along with all the ramifications that come with it. "We were in Malawi last November, the drought was palpable; we called on God, immediately rain fell. Rain shall fall for you!" We were in Arthur, India in 2014 and the drought was unimaginable; we cried to God, the heavens gave rain. Elijah said there is the sound of abundance of rain. Can you hear the sound?

> "We were in Malawi last November, the drought was palpable; we called on God, immediately rain fell. Rain shall fall for you!"

To you as an individual reading this piece, because of your covenant relationship with God the supernatural hand of God will work on your faith to deliver your divine supplies.

"In famine he shall redeem thee from death: and in war from the power of the sword. 21 Thou shalt be hid from the scourge of the tongue: neither shalt thou be afraid of destruction when it cometh. 22 At destruction and famine thou shalt laugh: neither shalt thou be afraid of the beasts of the earth." Job 5:20-22 BRG

That passage says that the Lord will take care of you so completely, that you will laugh in the face of destruction and famine. Start laughing right now!

Prayer: Oh Lord that has power to divinely supply, let me experience divine supply in all areas of need today in Jesus name.

Quotation: *The size of a challenge should never be measured by what we have to offer. It will never be enough. Furthermore, provision is God's responsibility, not ours. We are merely called to commit what we have - even if it's no more than a sack lunch."* —**Charles R. Swindoll**

6

Life Will Not Be Difficult
For You (Part 3)

PART C. *Engage In Prayer:*

> *"They shall not be ashamed in the evil time: and in the days of famine they shall be satisfied."* Psalm 37:19 BRG

Just a quick recap. In Parts 1 & 2 you saw that the situation globally is tough, as it was of old and you saw God made this pronouncement: that no matter how difficult things are, you will be cushioned from those devastating effects. To make that happen it was concluded there are three things you need to do: sow, expect divine supply and engage in prayer.

In the Christendom, God does not perform magic but miracles. Whereas magic is illusionary, miracles are supernatural. However, although the miraculous is in the realm of the supernatural it answers to the natural. How? All over the scripture you will hear God say: pray, ask, seek, knock, demand, command, call, supplicate, etc.; and in response to that, He changes the situation for your good.

It is in the realm of this that God is assuring us, that in the time of famine, if we will pray we will experience surplus.

"Do you know in these so called tough times, some people will become millionaires?"

I pray, you and I will receive the revelation that will get us there. This is the way it will happen, if you can pray it, you can get it.

> "Do you know in these so called tough times, some people will become millionaires?"

"Call unto me, and I will answer thee, and shew thee great and mighty things, which thou knowest not." Jeremiah 33:3 BRG

So, God is saying in the time of famine if you can 'pray' to me, I will show you the divine revelation that will take care of your needs. Note, I put pray in quotes above. In these days, what we call prayer is too shallow.

I recall about twenty years ago, I needed God to show me something about the trajectory of my life. I was fasting, working and studying the Bible, but the answer did not come. Then I went to Babalola Memorial Camp in Akareji, Nigeria, to wait on the Lord in fasting and prayer for seven days. Even while I was there on the mount, five days passed, no revelation.

One afternoon, I got tired and was just sauntering on the mount. I met a lady who also came to pray. After pleasantries, she inquired why I was on the mountain. I said, I wanted God to talk to me on a subject I consider very important in moving my destiny forward. But, God was not speaking. She laughed and said: "Is it that God is not speaking or, you were not listening?" Then she showed me a scripture that changed my prayer life forever. I hope it will change yours:

Psalm 19:1-2 KJV *"The heavens declare the glory of God and the firmament sheweth his handiwork. Day unto day uttereth speech, and night unto night sheweth knowledge."*

In essence, she showed me that God was speaking and I was not listening. Do you know our prayer meetings are the least attended nowadays? That despite all the knowledge of its benefit, instructions on how to do it and pastor constantly admonishing us to pray, many do not pray? How then do they want to be satisfied in the time of famine? I challenge you to put prayer to work today to see if it will work or, not work for you.

Matt 19:26, Luke 1:37, Mark 10:27 have something in common: with God, all things are possible if we pray and expect in faith.

Surely, in this time of famine, you shall be satisfied.

Have a great week!

Prayer: Lord, as your child, I know life will not be difficult for me. Dispatch any difficulty in my life to an everlasting fire! Prosper my household in the time of famine and beyond.

Quotation: *"The function of prayer is not to influence God, but rather to change the nature of the one who prays"* -**Søren Kierkegaard**

7

Dealing With Filthy Garments (Part 1)

"Now Joshua (the high priest) was clothed with filthy (nauseatingly vile) garments and was standing before the Angel [of the Lord]. Zechariah 3:3

It is said, that those who grow in knowledge are people who read and ask hard questions. The question you need to ask today is "What are the filthy garments on me?"

- ◆ Spiritually, what are those impure garments?
- ◆ What are those garments that are nauseatingly vile?
- ◆ Those garments, that will not allow me to get to my land that flows with milk and honey; my land of prosperity?
- ◆ What irritates people about me?
- ◆ What repels people around me?
- ◆ What have I put upon myself that is impure?

> "What is in my DNA that is denying my progress?"

- ◆ What has the enemy put upon me that is impure?
- ◆ What has sin put upon me that now defiles me?
- ◆ What has the world and worldly systems put upon me that makes me filthy?
- ◆ "What is in my DNA that is denying my progress?"
- ◆ What is the act of wickedness I am swimming in that is nauseatingly repulsive?
- ◆ What character do I have that irritates God and man?: Anger, bitterness, hatred, unforgiveness, stinginess, envy, greed, lack of contentment, corruption, etc.

Check these Bible characters out: Why could Cain not stand to see

Abel excel? What of Joseph's brothers being more concerned with how to destroy him than with their own careers? Why was David not satisfied with his numerous wives? Why was the prodigal son so greedily uncomfortable in the family?

Ask yourself, what is on me that will not allow me to succeed, prosper, and excel, academically, spiritually, materially, financially, physically, mentally, and health-wise this year!? Deal with them now, before they deal with you. How to deal with them is in the Bible, search it out!

Prayer: Every filthy garment on me, I remove you now in Jesus name. I wash myself in the blood of Jesus.

Quotation: *"I marvel to think that the Son of God would condescend to save us, as imperfect, impure, mistake-prone, and ungrateful as we often are. I have tried to understand the Savior's Atonement with my finite mind, and the only explanation I can come up with is this: God loves us deeply, perfectly, and everlastingly."* **-Dieter F. Uchtdorf**

8

Dealing With Filthy Garments (Part 2)

"Now Joshua (the high priest) was clothed with filthy (nauseatingly vile) garments and was standing before the Angel [of the Lord]". Zechariah 3:3 AMP

1. **Identify the impure garments**. A problem identified is half solved. Identify the filthy garments as we have done in Part One of this series, both your internal and external filthy garments. What are things in your life that you do that make you uncomfortable? Things you consider a reproach in your life. Troubling thoughts. That problem/challenge that everybody knows you have.

2. **Let Jesus handle Satan**. Secure the name of Jesus to deal with Satan in your life. Some of the filthy garments Satan has put upon you cannot be removed by you. You can cast out demons you cannot cast out Satan. It is not scripturally given to you to rebuke Satan. There is no need praying unscriptural prayers.
    But, thank God the one who drove him out of heaven can.
    "And the LORD said unto Satan, The LORD rebuke thee, O Satan; even the LORD that hath chosen Jerusalem rebuke thee: is not this a brand plucked out of the fire?" Zech 3:2 [KJV]
    Your prayer is like this, where you see Jerusalem in verse 2 put your name there. Continue the prayer by speaking out loud:
    "Over Amos Dada and this matter of reproach...Thy Lord rebuke you Satan." Cry as if everything around you depends on it: The Lord rebuke you Satan. Over the matter of: barrenness, failure, stagnation, limitation, anger, poverty, joblessness, immigration papers, bitterness, hatred, unforgiveness, murmuring, gossiping, stinginess, envy, immoral acts, greediness, lack of contentment, procrastination, corruption, party spirit, prayerlessness,

faithlessness, lack of self-control, time mismanagement –The Lord rebuke you Satan.

3. **Carry out self deliverance**: Then with great determination and meaningful purpose, begin to deal spiritually and practically with each filthy garment. Take unforgiveness as a case. As you finish reading this piece. Call the person that you know has offended you and you have been harbouring offense for sleeplessly on your bed. Don't go into details - just say sister/brother, so and so over this matter where you have offended me I forgive you. Go ahead make the call now! And regain your peace.

4. **Use an external resource person.** *"And he answered and spake unto those that stood before him, saying, Take away the filthy garments from him. And unto him he said, Behold, I have caused thine iniquity to pass from thee, and I will clothe thee with change of raiment."* Zech 3:4 KJV. That means you need assistance to take some filthy garments away. Who is standing before you, could be your Pastor, parents, deliverance minister or your prayer partner or even your spouse. Tell him/her I need you to pray with me over this matter. After the prayer: believe God has forgiven you your sins, and given you a change of garment.

5. **Prophesy to yourself your new status**. Say it loud. "Shame is gone from me." "Barrenness is gone from me." Tell yourself the evil garment is gone.

6. **Believe it is done**. You are free! No filthy garment of shame anymore. Continue to serve God with passion. Walk in your new of status. It is your year to prosper. Selah. Celebrate!

Let us take two more examples of filthy garments. The garment of anger and adultery.

1. **The issue of anger**: I was invited to minister in a church several years ago in London, England. After the ministration, a lady approached me. These are her words paraphrased: 'Pastor my husband loves me and I know and I love him too. But we are always quarreling. When he makes any small complaint I blow it out of proportion. My deep anger always flares up! By the time he says

one thing I have said ten. I need you to minister deliverance to me.' I told her "it is not every time you need to pray 'fire' prayers to secure your deliverance, counselling may be a cure." I narrated a story of a woman who had a similar problem

> "it is not every time you need to pray 'fire' prayers to secure your deliverance, counselling may be a cure."

and approached a herbalist for a solution. The herbalist said she should return in seven days. She complied. The herbalist said, whenever your husband complains again, just put this little item wrapped in cellophane in the corner of your mouth and keep quiet. She complied. Anytime the husband is out with his tantrum she will sneak to the toilet and put her 'charm' in her mouth. After two weeks the husband noticed there were no more quarrels and she commended her efforts. She returned to Herbalist to give thanks to him for a charm that 'worked' The herbalist said. I did not give you any charm. I only wrapped a small charcoal in the cellophane. Learn to keep quiet. Many of our filthy garments will disappear if we put our mouth in lock and key. Eating and speaking could be very dangerous. Manage your mouth and you will manage your health and your life.

2. **Let us take the issue of adultery**: Know that one day your secret will be exposed. See the shame and disgrace you will bring to yourself and maybe your family, career and ministry. Be content with your spouse. If you are a frequent traveler control your libido. Filthiness is tantamount to captivity. Ask the Lord to turn around your captivity by removing your filthiness.

Prayer: Lord, I thank you for giving me a new pure garment. I thank you for cleaning me up!

Quotation: *"I made a covenant with mine eyes; why then should I think upon a maid?"* **–Job 31:1**

9

You Are The Moses Of This Generation (Part 1)

PART A. *You Are Sent*

"*Then the LORD told him, "I have certainly seen the oppression of my people in Egypt. I have heard their cries of distress because of their harsh slave drivers. Yes, I am aware of their suffering. 8 So I have come down to rescue them from the power of the Egyptians and lead them out of Egypt into their own fertile and spacious land. It is a land flowing with milk and honey—the land where the Canaanites, Hittites, Amorites, Perizzites, Hivites, and Jebusites now live. 9 Look! The cry of the people of Israel has reached me, and I have seen how harshly the Egyptians abuse them. 10 Now go, for I am sending you to Pharaoh. You must lead my people Israel out of Egypt.*" - Exodus 3:7-10

> "Anybody that is not a Christian, is in a form of darkness, and bondage even though they may have a glorious future."

"*Then said Jesus to them again, 'Peace be unto you: as my Father hath sent me, even so, send I you.*" - John 20:21 KJV

Reader, you are chosen. Reader. you are sent.

((Anybody that is not a Christian, is in a form of darkness, and bondage even though they may have a glorious future.))

The unbeliever, is analogous to the Israelites under the bondage of their taskmasters in Egypt. Satan is daily oppressing them, using the word that God used when he wanted to rescue the Israelites. They are in distress. Satan torments them with sickness and diseases. With unwholesome lifestyles he burdens and sends them to an early grave. God says 'Satan harshly abuses them.'

But the good news is, God says 'I have heard their cries.'

God wants you to lead them out of Egypt, to their fertile and spacious land. A land flowing with milk and honey.

Will you be like Moses and complain? Moses gave eleven reasons why he could not go and do God's job.

At a point, God was so annoyed he wanted to kill him but, changed his mind and spared his life.

God met all the conditions and answered all the questions of Moses and empowered Moses.

Verse 12- says God put his words in the mouth of Moses.

Verse 21 -says God put his wonders in the hand of Moses.

God does not call the qualified. He qualifies the called. Those who are available.

Moses went and delivered the people. Reader, you are the Moses of this generation.

You are sent. You may not be able to deliver 2 million people but you may be able to deliver one. There is great joy in heaven over one sinner that repents. Leave Midian now (where you have been trained for X years) and head to Egypt to deliver God's people from bondage, and lead them to the land that flows with milk and honey- the CHRISTIAN LIFE!

It is time to evangelize. Go now! Stop giving excuses - go now! The field is ripe to be harvested. John 4:35

Stop procrastinating -go now! Stop hesitating -go now!

Stop the merry go round -go now! Save someone from hell fire! Jude 1:23 Just do it! Jesus is Lord.

Prayer. Lord thank you for sending me. Enable me to go and do exploits in your name.

Quotation: *"Why is it that some Christians cross land and sea, continents and cultures as missionaries? What on earth impels them? It is not in order to commend a civilization, an institution or an ideology, but rather a person, Jesus Christ, whom they believe to be unique."* — **John R.W. Stott**

10

You Are The Moses Of This Generation (Part 2)

PART B. *Reject What Can Hinder You*

> *"It was by faith that Moses when he grew up, refused to be called the son of Pharaoh's daughter. 25 He chose to share the oppression of God's people instead of enjoying the fleeting pleasures of sin. 26He thought it was better to suffer for the sake of Christ than to own the treasures of Egypt, for he was looking ahead to his great reward"* Hebrew 11:24-26

Moses, by his chosen lifestyle and decisions, like many heroes and heroines of Hebrews Chapter Eleven helped us to understand that faith goes beyond 'claiming this and claiming that' in the name of Christianity.

Moses grew up and refused certain things. Faith is about growing up and becoming a giant for God; leaving 'boyish' status to 'sonship'. I encourage you to study the phenomenon that is faith through my book "What is Faith?"

You will not be able to win souls for Christ, if you don't grow up. Babies always look unto their parents for food and things. Sons take care of the need of their parents. Those who attain great heights in life, have an unbelievably long list of what they refused. For example, Joseph refused Mrs. Potiphar's sexual advances; David refused to kill the anointed Saul; Job refused to curse God despite loss of fortune and 10 children; Jabez refused to blame his mother for calling him 'pain.'

However, Samson did not refuse the lure of Delilah's seductive eyes and his own eyes were plucked out. Those who want to maintain good health must refuse to eat junk. What are you refusing, so that you can grow up to be a mighty man of valour?

What are you refusing, so that you can win your generation for Christ? There are some companies you must learn to refuse!

Moses was not finished yet. In verse 25 - 'he chose' to share oppression. Another version says he chose to suffer affliction.

> "Friend, you need to choose suffering as part of the gospel to be able to affect your generation."

"Friend, you need to choose suffering as part of the gospel to be able to affect your generation."

You must choose to discipline yourself, your appetite. For your marriage to work, you must choose to suffer for your family. For that ministry and your church to grow, you must choose to suffer for Christ- it is still part of faith. For your nation to develop, you must choose to suffer for that nation. Moses chose not to enjoy the pleasure of sin. Paul chose to suffer for Christ. 2 Cor 11:21-33

You cannot be a masterpiece and an instrument of change for your community if, you continue to crave for sinful pleasures.

In verse 26, Moses 'thought it better' to suffer for Christ. As you read this piece, think of what you can do to advance the course of Christ and humanity. Don't just be a consumer of other people's thoughts, think through some things that will help this generation. Take the high road though it may be a narrow road. Do what God will be pleased and happy with. That is not only faith, it is evangelism.

Finally, Moses was looking ahead to a great reward.

Follow the sequence, grow, refuse, choose and have a good thought and do the work of evangelism.

There is a great reward we are looking forward to! Friend, it will not be long; the great rewarder will reward you. The strategy of Moses will work any day any time for anyone anywhere on planet earth. Jesus is Lord!

Prayer: Help me to follow the sequence, grow, refuse, choose and have a good thought and do the work of evangelism. O' Lord in the words of Nehemiah remember me for good.

Quotation: *"You recognize the truth because sometimes it's hard to swallow, but if you hold it in your mouth, refusing to eat it, you are going to choke."* **-Monica Johnson**

11

You are the Moses of this generation (Part 3)

PART C. *Give God The Credit*

> *"Moses told his father-in-law'(Jethro)' everything the Lord had done to Pharaoh and Egypt on behalf of Israel. He also told about all the hardships they had experienced along the way and how the Lord had rescued his people from all their troubles."* Exodus 18:8-9 NLT

In Part 2 of this series, we saw how Moses used personal discipline to accomplish great feats in his personal life and ministry. There is no alternative to self-development. If you want to climb the ladder of life to success, look inwards before looking outwards. If you have done your math, your excellent result is a function of time. Success they say is always the best revenge. You don't argue with positive results. Let us learn about the communication skills of Moses. Like David, we saw Moses counting all his blessing (Psalm103). Moses was the one whom God used to face the no- nonsense, hard - hearted, task master Pharaoh in Egypt. He was the one throwing down the rod and that rod became a snake; he was the one the people saw, who said 'let water turn to blood' and it was so. Let frogs invade the whole land of Egypt, and Pharaoh's bedroom will not be spared. Yet, in narrating his story, he told his father-in-law 'everything the Lord had done to Pharaoh', learn to give the credit of your human achievements to whom it belongs- God. In John 15:5- Jesus says without me you can do nothing. Do you remember what you said, when you were giving testimony in church? Everything is about you. I prayed. I fasted. I paid my tithe. I gave to the poor. I, I, I… Slow down. You can do all that, and if God does not allow the result to be positive, you will still have no testimony. Learn to give God the credit. He deserves it.

> "I have good news for you this week, God will rescue you from all your troubles."

"I have good news for you this week, God will rescue you from all your troubles." God will give you a fresh start, no matter your idiosyncrasies (personal style, approach to things).

You will tell stories of victories. You will tell stories of God's mercies.

You will tell stories of joy, successes, and promotion. You will tell stories of God's greatness.

Jethro brought back Moses's wife and sons to him in the wilderness.

You will tell stories of great reunion, family reunion, success and great exploits in Jesus name.

No more stories of distress, disdain, debt, depression and all the evil ' Dees' but, the stories of God's ultimate triumph. Your story has changed. Glory to God.

"Praise the Lord," Jethro said, "for he has rescued you from the Egyptians and from Pharaoh. Yes, he has rescued Israel from the powerful hand of Egypt! 11 I know now that the Lord is greater than all other gods because he rescued his people from the oppression of the proud Egyptians." Ex 18:10

Thy Lord will rescue you also, even your in-laws will join in the celebration in Jesus name.

But you must learn to give God the credit, the glory.

Prayer: Teach me O' Lord to realise that without you I can do nothing and that for all my successes to give you the credit.

Quotation *"Our voices, our service, and our abilities are to be employed, primarily, for the glory of God."* - **Billy Graham**

12

You Are The Moses Of This Generation (Part 4)

PART C. *Your In-Law Is A Blessing*

> *"The next day, Moses took his seat to hear the people's disputes against each other. They waited before him from morning till evening.14 When Moses' father-in-law saw all that Moses was doing for the people, he asked, "What are you really accomplishing here? Why are you trying to do all this alone while everyone stands around you from morning till evening?"17 "This is not good!" Moses' father-in-law exclaimed. 18 "You're going to wear yourself out—and the people, too. This job is too heavy a burden for you to handle all by yourself. 19 Now listen to me, and let me give you a word of advice, and may God be with you. You should continue to be the people's representative before God, bringing their disputes to him. 20 Teach them God's decrees, and give them his instructions. Show them how to conduct their lives. 21 But select from all the people some capable, honest men who fear God and hate bribes. Appoint them as leaders over groups of one thousand, one hundred, fifty, and ten."* Exodus 18:13-21 [NLT]

Let us learn some relationship and leadership skills from Moses. First lesson, not all in-laws are evil. May God give you good in-laws who are interested in your success. If in the natural, your in-laws cannot just get along with you, or, sorry, you cannot get along with your in-laws - turn it to prayers. Pray like this, 'You made Jethro a blessing to Moses, O Lord, make my Jethro's a major blessing to me.'

Jethro was interested in the affairs of his son-in-law, and wasn't afraid to share words of wisdom. You know he could have kept quiet. You know he could have been grumbling with his daughter, condemning Moses. He could have even blamed the daughter for marrying such an unskillful man. He could have found all the but offered no solution. Instead, he came with words of wisdom. Moses, on the other hand, could have easily snubbed Jethro. You are old fashioned, old man all you know is about sheep, do you want to compare sheep to human beings? Are you not familiar with that? Just try to correct your children or, the youth in your church and you are told, man, you don't get it, this is a computer, technology, social media age, you are old school! You are not current. This is a modern world. It is not as you think. Moses appreciated the wisdom of the Elders. No wonder he lived for 120 years and his eyes were still sharp. "May God help you to recognize your divine and destiny helper."

Jethro encouraged Moses to learn the principle of delegating authority. He obliged. I encourage you to do some delegation in your church, office, school. Build bridges. Stop the age old in-law war. Watch the *War Room* movie. We could all always use some advice, and somethimes the best comes from the most unlikely of places. My father in-law would say, two good heads are better than one. You do not have a monopoly of knowledge. In-laws are not threats to your marriage, approach them with wisdom. In-laws build your children's marriages, help them to succeed, stop the blame game, stop taking sides.

Some words of Elders are words of wisdom, use them!

Prayer: O' Lord help me to handle my in-laws. Let me learn from them. Let my in-laws not be my enemies but friend to our homes.

Quotation: *"A mother gives you a life, a mother-in-law gives you her life."* — **Amit Kalantri**

13

What Is God Telling You To Do First?

"But Elijah said to her, "Don't be afraid! Go ahead and do just what you've said, but make a little bread for me first. Then use what's left to prepare a meal for yourself and your son. 14 For this is what the Lord, the God of Israel, says: There will always be flour and olive oil left in your containers until the time when the Lord sends rain and the crops grow again!" I King 17:13-14 TLB

The story is well known and well rehearsed. The question is: 'What is the significance of the story?' To me, it is a survival strategy in a time of serious adversity. It could also be called, strategy for prosperity in the time of want and scarcity. "God's principle is clear, do mine first and I will do yours." Serving God is about the relationship. It's about trust. Jesus said: *"But seek ye first the kingdom of God and His righteousness, and all these things shall be added to you."* Matt 6:33

> "God's principle is clear, do mine first and I will do yours."

In Job 42: He told Job 'pray for your friends first' and, watch what happens. God is a God of order.

Put me first and watch what happens next. The big question is: "What has God told you to do first?"

To the widow of Zarephath: 'make a little bread for me first.'

♦ Go and bring bread to me first.
♦ Go and give to that orphanage first.
♦ Go and repent of your sins first.
♦ Go and reconcile to that aggrieved person first, before bringing your offering and tithe to me.
♦ Go and pray for that sister, brother, friend, neighbour, Pastor first.

- ♦ Go and evangelise first. Go and be a witness first.
- ♦ Go and repent first.
- ♦ Go and forgive that church member, family member, Pastor and that colleague first.
- ♦ Go and apologize to your wife/ husband/parent/children/Uncle/ Aunty, first.
- ♦ Go and bless that man/woman of God first. Go and study your book first before boy/girlfriend affair.
- ♦ Go and marry first before sexual relationship.
- ♦ Go and register in that school first. Go and finish your degree first.
- ♦ Go and withdraw that divorce papers first. Go and encourage that brother/sister first.
- ♦ Go and return to that church you left in anger because you don't want to be under authority.
- ♦ Go back to your first love of Christ, where you delighted in the Word of God, prayer, and fellowship.
- ♦ Go and find out what you are to do first and do it and watch God turn your situation around.

Jesus is Lord!

Prayer: O' Lord, help me to do the necessary things first.

Quotation. *"Start by doing what's necessary; then do what's possible; and suddenly you are doing the impossible."* — **Francis of Assisi**

14

What Is Your Report Card Like?

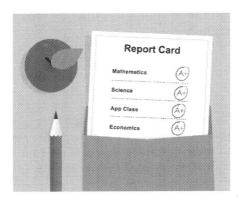

"But prove yourselves doers of the word, and not merely hearers who delude themselves. 23 For if anyone is a hearer of the word and not a doer, he is like a man who looks at his natural face in a mirror; 24 for once he has looked at himself and gone away, he has immediately forgotten what kind of person he was." James 1:22-24 [NASB]

One of the advantages of the calendar is, that it helps you to see the beginning and the end. The beginning of a day, week, month and year. A calendar when properly used helps you to know you have ended a chapter and you are beginning another chapter. So, one of the best ways to use the calendar is to be able to evaluate what you have done within a period and to plan for the beginning of another period. Where I am going is that, you should be able to sit down at the end of every year and do a personal evaluation. Evaluate yourself, and that exercise should help you plan a trajectory, of what you want to do and where you want to go, and hope to achieve in the year ahead. Evaluation is not meant to condemn you or, make you depressed if you did not achieve your planned objectives in the outgoing period. It is to help you re-strategize.

While preparing this, I read about a girl that failed grade 12 (WAEC) five times and eventually made a First Class degree later. Look out for where you have 'failed' or, if that word is too strong for you, where you did not 'measure up' and find out why and make amends. Women do a physical evaluation every day when they use the mirror. They correct what they feel is inappropriate on their face, and apply more cosmetics where necessary. They got the principle from the Bible.

"But prove yourselves doers of the word, and not merely hearers who delude themselves. 23For if anyone is a hearer of the word and not a doer, he is like a man who looks at his natural face in a mirror; 24 for once he has looked at himself and gone away, he has immediately forgotten what kind of person he was" James 1:22-24 NASB

Pastor Dada what course(s) will I be evaluated on? I will tell you. Evangelism, faithfulness, church, bible study, prayer meeting attendance, giving to the gospel, prayer, witnessing, intercession, hospitality, prison ministry, missions and tithing. Where did you score A or F. Evaluation should not be limited to your faces alone. It should be extended to your total physical, mental and spiritual being. Have you gained excessive weight and increased your BMI due to overeating or, eating the wrong stuff or, due to lack of discipline to exercise? Have you ignored prayer, reading and meditating on scriptures and fellowship? What of your financial status? How did you make money and how did you spend it? Have you spent your money, or invested your money? If you expended your money on frivolities and prostitutes, you have spent your money. If you expended your money on your family, taking care of your spouse, paying your children school fees, given to charity, helping the needy donating to the church, paying your tithe, you have invested your money.

As a youth, how have you spent your year? How have you managed your time? One of the time wasters of our time is the social media. Whereas the smart few are designing various social media Apps, and doing online businesses and smiling to the bank; over 99 percent of the users are wasting away. You must be able to find out, how many hours you are expending daily on your Facebook, LinkedIn, Twitter, etc. If the usage is bringing revenue to you fine, but if it is just waking up to showcase the x-ray of your three-month pregnancy, then you need to examine yourself. I was in Nigeria for about three weeks this December, and I saw how much money was being wasted on unnecessary telephone conversations. These are the people who claimed they have no job and money. Unlike North America, where you have a plan and pay fix amount of money on telephone bills, the African market is hugely different and exploited. I traveled from Tanzania to Malawi, Kenya, and Ghana before arriving in Nigeria. I saw how the telecommunications gurus are exploiting Africans. Still, you cannot blame them, you are not forced to buy airtime. It is out of your indiscretion that you waste your money on those calls. There is an adage that says, you may not be able to prevent a bird from flying over your head but you can prevent it from building a nest.

What I really want to focus on today is, your spiritual assessment and personal evaluation. Your ability to spiritually position yourself, will determine how far you can go in life. This is emphasised by the famous scripture on prosperity:

"Beloved, I wish above all things that thou mayest prosper and be in health, even as thy soul prospereth." 3 John 1:2 KJV

One of the most important principles that guides the way, and what I preach comes from 2 Corinthians 3:18 NASB It says, *"...we all, with unveiled face beholding as in a mirror the glory of the Lord, are being transformed into the same image from glory to glory, just as from the Lord, the Spirit."* The principle is this: true gospel change of a person's character comes from steady gazing at the glory of Jesus. "Beholding the glory of the Lord, we are being transformed into his image." We become like what we treasure enough, to spend time focusing on. Some say, "Seeing is believing." This text says, "Seeing is becoming." You become like what you behold.

The implication of this for preaching is that, if I aim for us as a church to be transformed from one degree of glory to another—to become more and more like Jesus—then I should hold up Jesus again and again for you to gaze at. We need to see Jesus.

There are things about Christ, that we need very much at the end of this year. We need the perseverance of Christ in the face of affliction. We need the energy and strength of Christ in the face of global aggressive pressures. We need the wisdom of Christ in the face of complexities of life and ministry. We need the stability of Christ in the midst of rapid social, political and personal changes all around us.

We need the assurance of His sovereign authority, in a culture sliding farther and farther from His truth.

((It is no exaggeration to say that we need Christ in the totality

of our lives)). 1 John 3:2 says, *"Beloved, we are God's children now. It does not yet appear what we shall be. But we know that when he appears we shall be like him for we shall see him as he is."* To the degree that we can see him now, we are changed into his image. When he comes to be seen in his full glory, our transforming will be completed. And it all happens because of seeing Him—gazing steadily at Him.

The question is, how much of Jesus have you in the beginning of the year and how much of Him have you now? Have you gyrated towards him better or, have you drifted away from him altogether or, are you just stagnant in one spot? If you have attended service every Sunday this year then, you have heard an average of 52 sermons. What is the impact of 52 sermons on your life? Are you just a hearer or are you a doer?

The story of Mordecai in Esther Chapter 6 comes handy. Mordecai was serving a king that could be said not to be a Christian, but he Mordecai, was a Christian and he served the king in the integrity of his heart. Some people plotted to kill King Ahasuerus. Mordecai did not only refuse to be involved in the assassination plot but also reported the people. He was not looking for a reward, but doing his normal service. How have you performed your service in this year?

Have you been involved in destroying people, despite the fact that Psalm 1 encouraged you not be a scorner? Have you slept with another man's wife? Have you slept with another woman's husband?

Have you destroyed a young woman's future by your infidelity? As a young man have you impregnated a young woman and colluded to carry out an abortion? As a young woman have you lost your virginity and womanhood virtue to a careless sugar coated young man who is gong no where life? Or have you sold your virtue to secure a job? Have you cheated in your exams? Are you involved in any corruption at any level? Did you give bribe or take bribe in the course of the year? Have you abused the trust your nation entrusted you with? Did you inflate contracts and share the loot and thereby oppressed the poor? Are you part of the terrorist gang destroying churches, killing and maiming innocent children? What have you spent the year doing?

Mordecai was not only involved in protecting the king, he was defending the cause of the oppressed Jews. When nobody stood up against the aggression of Haman the influential Vice President, Mordecai came out strong; rallying his niece Esther the queen and all who could pray and fast to rescue a perishing nation. How have you delivered the oppressed in the outgoing year? Christians and Christianity have suddenly become the target of aggression in our time. You cannot preach the gospel as it is, you will be called names; if not imprisoned as well. In our time we see ISIS, Al-Shabaab, Boko Haram and other terrorist organizations slaughtering Christians in the hundreds. In some ridiculous cases, they will even show them on YouTube and other social media when they are being slaughtered! Have you been motivated to preach the gospel with fire and great zeal? How many souls have you won for Christ this year? What have you done to fight corruption? Or, are you part of corruption?

Have you helped the needy in your community? Or, were you preoccupied with your little challenges that you could not even count your blessings? Psalm 103 helps you to catalog all that God has done. As this year progress evaluate yourself.

The king Ahasuerus could not sleep until he blessed and rewarded Mordecai. While the wicked Haman was imagining that he will be the one to get the blessing, he was the one to parade Mordecai around the city shouting his praise. That tells you two things; firstly, God will still remember you and reward you before this year comes to an end. The King of Kings, The Lord of Lords, will reward you before this year ends. Secondly, your enemy will bring the blessing to you!

As you go to the New Year, I am holding up Jesus for you to look unto; the author and finisher of our faith. With you looking at the Master, trusting in the Master, protecting the interest of the Master, the King of Kings will surprise you in the New Year. All the good things you did and it seems no one noticed, guess what, it is in the book of life. God will reward you here and in the life to come.

"Then Peter began to say unto him, Lo, we have left all, and have followed thee. And Jesus answered and said, Verily I say unto you, There is no man that hath left house, or brethren, or sisters, or father, or mother, or wife, or children, or lands, for my sake, and the gospel's, But he shall receive an hundredfold now in this time, houses, and brethren, and sisters, and mothers, and children, and lands, with persecutions; and in the world to come eternal life." Mark 10;28-30 [KJV]

Prayer points:

1. Every spirit that negates my finishing well be destroyed in Jesus name.
2. Every spirit that nullifies people's glory, be destroyed in my life in Jesus name.
3. Disgrace all the Haman scheduled to disgrace me.
4. Assign my enemy to showcase my glory.
5. All my hidden blessings bring them out O Lord.
6. Lord, it is not too late to bless me, bless me now.
7. Lord open your book of remembrance for me.
8. Lord who opened the book of remembrance for Mary, for Mordecai and for Esther before this year ends, open my own.
9. Let me not receive bad news. Whatever is called bad news let it be far from me.
10. Lord before this year ends, put an end to my struggles, even internal struggles.
11. Lord, you rewarded Mordecai for his good deeds, hand over my rewards in Jesus name.
12. Lord turn my trials to testimonies.
13. Lord give me a break-through before this year ends.
14. Let the fire of God destroy every Haman planning my downfall and that of my family.

Prayer: I pray you and I shall not fail the exam of life in Jesus name.

Quotation: *"Life is like a book. Some chapters sad, some happy, and some exciting. But if you never turn the page. You will never know what the next chapter holds."* -**Unknown**

15

Signals You Are Growing Or Not Growing In The Lord?

"As newborn babes, desire the sincere milk of the word, that ye may grow thereby" 1 Peter 2:2

In science, engineering and most disciplines in the world, they talk about benchmarks. Let me apply this principle to spiritual growth, and share with you some benchmarks for spiritual growth. It is to help you, never to condemn you.

1. **DELIGHTING IN THE BIBLE**
    If reading the Bible is a struggle for you, you are not growing. But, if it is a delight for you, then there you grow! Transformation can be recognized in people when their minds are sharpened by the Bible. If your views and actions are not sharpened or, directed by the Bible you may debate it but, you are not growing. Psalm 1:3, Jos 1:8

2. **OBEYING GOD AND DENYING SELF**
    Do you love obeying God in all things or, just in areas you find convenient? Making God your Saviour and not Lord, is a way to know you are not growing. Enjoying God blessings is not

evidence of spiritual growth. People progressing in their faith prioritize God's desires over self-will, they delight in obeying Him 'in season and out of season'. Transformation is marked by your progressively setting aside earthly delights for Kingdom priorities. God's blessing is based on listening and obeying his commands- Deut 28:1-14. God's curses are based on not listening to him and disobeying him, Deut 15:68.What did you order for?

3. **SERVING GOD AND OTHERS**

Do you love serving people or, do you love being served? Watching messages on TV, YouTube, Facebook and other social media and not engaging yourself in any local assembly; where you are serving with your time, energy, finance, and talent is not a sign of spiritual growth. Even if you are in the church and you are not serving, guess what, you are a liability and not an asset. Just as Jesus said He had come to serve and not to be served, so must believers. Transformation is evident when personal needs, and even life goals, are set aside for the needs we see in others. Your prosperity is predicated on service, meeting the needs of others.

4. **SHARING CHRIST.**

Do you delight in sharing the gospel? Like Paul, do you have any burden or necessity to share the gospel of Jesus Christ? Jesus says my father works and I work. If you are not working witnessing, preaching, inviting people to Christ, being passionate and compassionate about it, you are not growing. Maturing believers know speaking about the message of Jesus is a necessity. Transformation is evident when we talk about the source. You are empowered by the Holy Spirit to be a witness. Period. Acts 1:8.

5. **AVOIDING SIN.**

"Do you still engage in continual acts of sin? He that covers his sin shall not prosper." You are not growing if you are deliberately engaging in sinful acts. If it is a snare to you and you are working with others to get it out that is a different matter. But to be living in sin and cover up with church activities, you are not growing.

> "Do you still engage in continual acts of sin? He that covers his sin shall not prosper."

Act 3:19. *If we deliberately keep on sinning after we have received the knowledge of the truth, no sacrifice for sins is left, 27 but only a fearful expectation of judgment and of raging fire that will consume the enemies of God.* Heb 10:26-27

6. **OTHERS**

   What is your faith level? Can you measure a person's faith? Probably not. But you can see it when it is put into action. Are you seeking God? People become Disciples of Christ because they intend to follow Him and become like Him. Are you building a relationship, as believers? Your horizontal relationships with others should develop just as your vertical relationship with God does. Are you ashamed of the gospel? The adage is "if you aim at nothing, you will hit it every time." At the very heart of Christianity is the work of making disciples for Christ. It should never sit at the fringe of your lives or the Church.

Prayer: Oh Lord help me to grow in you. I reject stagnation, in all forms.

Quotation: *"All growth depends upon activity. There is no development physically or intellectually without effort, and effort means work."* — **Calvin Coolidge** Permit me to add-even spiritual growth is work!

16

How To Handle Evil Thoughts

"For as he thinketh in his heart, so is he: Eat and drink, saith he to thee; but his heart is not with thee." Proverbs 23:7

"For the thing which I greatly feared is come upon me, and that which I was afraid of comes unto me." Job 3:25

There are many ways to handle evil thoughts. Whichever way you choose, make sure you do not allow evil thoughts to germinate. If it has germinated, it is a dangerous weed. Kill it now! What are evil thoughts? All thoughts that do not help your life in any way, are evil thoughts. Sometimes they are called temptations. They are offensive, bad, dangerous, unwholesome, ridiculous, ungodly thoughts. Here are some examples- not that you don't know: When you are thinking of hurting yourself, committing a sin, engaging in immoral acts, thinking of having sexual relationship outside your marriage, thinking of sleeping around, committing fornication, thinking you cannot make it, thinking you cannot pass that exam because you failed once, thinking that even when you finish school you will not get job, that you will die young, that your children might die before you, that you will die because of the sickness or, disease that has afflicted you, when having suicidal thoughts, to jump down from a skyscraper, hurting or harming someone else, killing your spouse because of insurance policy, snatching your friends spouse, that your booming business will just collapse for no reason, that your associate pastor will bolt away with the church members, that you are going to die in a vehicle/aircraft accident, that you cannot make it, giving up prematurely, engaging in diabolical and unethical ways to be rich/ prosperous, killing your boss to secure his/ her position, that your child can one day come home to introduce same-sex partner as a future life partner, that you can wake up one day and be diagnosed with cancer, high blood pressure, your spouse might suddenly drop dead and leave you as a widow/widower, that you are a failure, that your marriage will suffer shipwreck and make you a divorcee or separate, I guess the list has no end!

Here are some possible solutions in handling them:

1. Number one way is to rebuke them aloud at the source before they fester.

2. Research scriptures that can help you out of it. Meditate on it constantly. "When you fill your heart with the word of God you will not have room for negative thoughts." Read Phil 4.8, Psalm 119:11; Joshua 1:8

> "When you fill your heart with the word of God you will not have room for negative thoughts."

3. If you rebuke it as mentioned above and it persists, share it with someone. With your spouse, pastor, parent, guardian, a confidante, mentor, friend, someone that can help you not the one that will compound it. Call it your accountability partner.

4. Pray and fast about it. Don't treat it with kid's gloves. Don't contract it out. Pray about it yourself.

5. Still persisting, go for deliverance. By the grace of God, we can help you in deliverance.

Rebuke it and rebuke it aloud. The story was told of Baba Babajide, one time General Evangelist of Christ Apostolic Church Worldwide. One time, he came home with a couple of pastors and evangelists in training and bid them sit in his sitting room while he alone entered the inner room.

Suddenly, the pastors were hearing Papa shouting forcefully 'jade, mo ni ko jade' meaning 'Get out, I said get out'. When Papa came back to the sitting room, the pastors asked, sir, who were you addressing and talking to within the room? You are the only one that entered the room, sir! He replied - they are the evil thoughts, the thoughts that have no respect for your pastoral collar, they enter your thought realm without your permission. Don't entertain them. Deal with them decisively before they deal with you. Don't give them an inch because, they will take a yard if you do so.'

I have written two books about this issue of deliverance: **'Practical Guide to Destroying Curses and Evil Covenants'** and **'Turning Curses to Blessings'** also, listen/subscribe to my messages on YouTube under the channel DrAmosDada.

Whatever the case, instead of evil thoughts, think good thoughts. *"Finally, brethren, whatsoever things are true, whatsoever things are honest, whatsoever things are just, whatsoever things are pure, whatsoever things are lovely, whatsoever things are of good report; if there be any virtue, and if there be any praise, think on these things"* Phil 4:8

My prayer for you is, that you will not be a victim of your evil thoughts like Job. Take steps now. Don't learn from your mistakes; learn from other people's mistakes. That is how to live for Jesus in a month of living for Jesus. Jesus is Lord!

Prayer: In the name of Jesus I destroy the root of evil thoughts in my life.

Quotation: *"The world is a dangerous place to live, not because of the people who are evil, but because of the people who don't do anything about it."*
-Albert Einstein

17

Advice For Parents

"As for you, my son Solomon, know the God of your father, and serve Him with a whole heart and a willing mind; for the LORD searches all hearts, and understands every intent of the thoughts If you seek Him, He will let you find Him; but if you forsake Him, He will reject you forever." -1 Chronicles 28:9

Train up a child in the way he should go, Even when he is old he will not depart from it. -Proverbs 22:6

Stop running helter-skelter about what you will leave for your children. No. **Do your best to leave something good in them**. What you leave in them will grow; what you leave for them will depreciate.

My father did not go to school, he was not worth much financially. He left no appreciable property for me and my siblings. He, however, left education and Christ in me. In his old age, I built a house for him and was responsible for most of his clothing and feeding.

Stop stealing to enable you to leave wealth for your children. Stop teaching them to steal also, because, they will follow the example of what you do. In my book ***Dream Dreams and Have Dominion*** I wrote, warn your children like anything about the dangers of smoking. If you are smoking, a study by the Columbia University showed that your child is 3x more likely to also smoke.

Said in another way, "leave in them values, not valuables (material things). Invest in them, not for them. Be a role model for them."

> "leave in them values, not valuables (material things). Invest in them, not for them. Be a role model for them."

Don't say to your children do what I say not what I do! They will do what you are doing, no matter what you say.

Don't be a permissive parent or an absentee parent. Be there when they are young and train them in the way of the Lord. If your children are living with you and they are young take this counsel seriously. I am not against taking children for piano lessons and ballet training and similar extra-curriculum activities. But, let your preference be to take them to Sunday School, Bible Study and other channels, where they can be fed at an early stage with the word of God. Expose them to the knowledge of Christ in there formative years-before 5 years of age. The society is in trouble today particularly in the Western World because of lack of exposure to biblical principles. How will the youth not carry guns and shoot any one in school when they have not learnt about the fear of God and sanctity of life? Until biblical principles are restored to school as we are advocating, take your destiny in your hands and train your children in the way of God.

You shall teach them to your sons, talking of them when you sit in your house and when you walk along the road and when you lie down and when you rise up. Deuteronomy 11:9

Lastly, teach them to develop their inner qualities rather than their outward appearances.

Prayer: Help me to be a good parent and to leave a good and godly legacy for my children.

Quotation: *"You have the right to mess up your own life, but you don't have the right to mess up your child's life."* -**Unknown**

18

Why You Need Jesus-
The Claims Of Jesus.

"If this is so, then the Lord knows how to rescue the godly from trials and to hold the unrighteous for punishment on the Day of Judgment." 2 Peter 2:9

There are three categories of people you can live for: yourself, Satan or Jesus. The following should help you decide who to live for:

1. Jesus claimed to be God when He took the Name of God, "I am that I am", revealed in Ex 3:14 and applied it to Himself (See John 8:58). You need the I AM in your life.

2. Jesus claimed to have the authority to forgive sins (see Matt 9:6) something only God can do.
   Thank God for the redemption of our soul through the shedding of His blood.

3. Jesus claimed that anyone who believes in Him would live forever with Him (John 3:16, 11:25-26). After death, there is another life in hell or, heaven.

4. Jesus claimed that anyone who does not believe that He is the "I am" would "die in their sins" John 8:24. You don't have to die in your sin anymore.

> "I am the Way the Truth and The Life."

5. Jesus claimed to be the only path through which any human could come into relationship with the true God! (John 10:9, 14:6). "I am the Way the Truth and The Life."

6. Jesus claimed to be the personal Judge of every individual, and that He alone would ultimately decide their destiny after death.

7. Jesus claimed he will return; "you shall see me coming in the clouds" Mark 14:62, Matt 26:64, 2 Tim 4:8. Are you ready for the coming of the Master?

In the season of Living for Jesus, these claims are not only unique to the Master, they are 'heavy'. They decide how you will enjoy the earth and eternity.

I love Jesus and I enjoy everything about Him. That is why I am living for him.

Learn to enjoy Him too. Have a great week! Jesus is Lord.

Prayer: O' Lord you made some salient claims. Help me to see the value in your claims and live for you.

Quotation: *"I am the Way, the Truth, and the Life. No one comes to the Father except through me. Do not let your hearts be troubled. Trust in God; trust also in Me."* **-Jesus Christ**

19

How To Lose Paradise

The Case Study of Eve & Adam

> *"And when the woman saw that the tree was good for food and that it was pleasant to the eyes, and a tree to be desired to make one wise, she took of the fruit thereof, and did eat, and gave also unto her husband with her; and he did eat."*
> Gen 3:6

Note: Paradise, in the context of this spiritual and intellectual discourse is used literally (heavenly paradise) and figuratively or, symbolically (marriage, job, ministry, career, business, etc.). Do the following and lose:

1. Listen to Satan's suggestions, gossips, murmurings always and not to God.(Refuse to read the Bible)
2. Engage Satan and his cohorts and subordinates in conscious arguments or, useless and baseless discussions.
3. Ignore God's instruction through the Bible (his commands), his direct words to you and through the prophets and ministers.
4. Value what Satan says over what God says or, better said, believe what Satan says rather than God.
5. Always look for food that can destroy you. Bear in mind sex is food. Love what God hates.
6. Continue to encourage your spouse to disobey God in every regards especially in tithing, fellowship, prayer, giving and many other ways.
   "Blame everybody for all your mistakes except yourself."
7. Refuse to repent when God prompts you about your sinful, offensive and inappropriate misbehaviours.
8. Forget that God made you put you in paradise and has power to throw

"Blame everybody for all your mistakes except yourself."

you out of paradise; no matter your reasoning, logic and futile arguments.

9. Refuse to learn from mistakes of others,; wait foolishly to learn from your own mistakes.
10. Continue to disobey God and continue to collect curses instead of blessings.
11. Continue to disobey God and start parking out of paradise behaving as if disobedience to God has no consequences.

God forbid!

Be wise. Ponder on this and remain in paradise on earth and gain entrance to heavenly paradise.

Prayer: O' Lord let me not loose paradise in Jesus name.

Quotations: *"He who indulges in falsehood will find the paths of paradise shut to him."* **- Anonymous**

20

May You Finish Well!

"And I ask you, my true partner, to help these two women, for they worked hard with me in telling others the Good News. They worked along with Clement and the rest of my co-workers, whose names are written in the Book of Life." - Philemon 4:3

The starting point is not always the same for everyone, except that we were all born naked. But the desire to finish well and strong is the same. Everyone desires to finish well. I pray you will finish well.

I trust that you have done all you could to finish this year well. I thank God for giving you the grace of life. Life is one thing, as much as you have input on how you live, the ultimate decision on when you shall take your exit is the giver of life-God. Since it has pleased him to keep you till this hour, I pray he will help you many more.

Just as Paul discusses above, my prayer is that our names are written in the book of life.

We have laboured in our various ministries, attending services, giving offerings and tithes, preaching the gospel in season and out of season. I even remember some in my church, Christ Apostolic Church Bethel Toronto, leaving in groups during services this year to preach in the malls and streets. It is the grace of God. On the platform of International Gathering of Eagles-how many 'Clements' can I remember in 12 nations where we held the conference in one year? Not many. But my prayer is that you will finish well.

Let us gear up with the great vision and even greater vigor and zeal. Not just to finish the work of the Master anyhow or, somehow but to finish well. To finish strong.

Saul the king, Solomon the man who wrote so well about wisdom, Samson the highly anointed all had questionable ends. You don't want that, neither do I. Paul was confident not only of the Clements whose names are written in the book of life, but of himself-' I have fought a good fight. I have finished my course, awaiting me is the crown of life'. I pray we all crossover to The New Year and crossover many more years if the Lord tarries. Let us remember, one day we shall not just crossover to a new year with all the euphoria and excitement, but, we shall one day at a time crossover to eternity. That is where it really matters. Those who cross over to eternity with Christ have finished well and those on the other side called hell have not finished well.

> *"How you lived in the past, how you are living now, and how you will live till you die, will be part of your final report card."*

"How you lived in the past, how you are living now, and how you will live till you die, will be part of your final report card." Let it be your desire to make every year, a year you shall live well and finish well. I ask you, my true partner, to help others and me to finish well. Therefore, let the crossover that matters, be the crossover to heaven with the Lord.

How do you finish well?

By faithfully carrying out the following:

- ♦ Daily time of focused personal communion with God.
- ♦ Daily living of the gospel.
- ♦ Daily commitment to God as a living sacrifice.
- ♦ Daily commitment to your family, career, and fellowship.
- ♦ Firm belief in the sovereignty and love of God.
    - ○ According to Paul they exhibit the following characteristics:
    - ○ They leave behind one or more ultimate contributions.

- o Truth is lived out in their lives so that convictions and promises of god are seen to be real
- o They manifest Christ-likeness in character as evidenced by the fruit of the spirit in their lives.
- o They maintain a learning posture and can learn from various kinds of sources— life especially
- o They maintain a personal vibrant relationship with god right up to the end.
- o They walk with a growing awareness of a sense of destiny and see some or all of it fulfilled.

Prayer: O' Lord let me finish well in the bosom of the Lord in the year.

Quotation: *"No matter who you are or what you do, embrace the challenge to first start with the goal to finish strong."* – **Andy Andrews**

21

If God Does Not Kill You No One Can-The Case Study Of Donald Trump.

"I returned and saw under the sun, that the race is not to the swift, nor the battle to the strong, neither yet bread to the wise, nor yet riches to men of understanding, nor yet favour to men of skill; but time and chance happeneth to them all".
Ecclesiastes 9:11

"By all means, I am not a self-styled prophet. I do not see people's intestines, bank accounts, phone numbers (thank God for those that see that far) but, I know I hear God." By the grace of God, every Dec 31st I release prophetic utterances generally for the church and nations. Those in CAC Bethel will recall that God told me concerning the election in America in 2016 - there will be a lot of surprises.

> "By all means, I am not a self-styled prophet. I do not see people's intestines, bank accounts, phone numbers (thank God for those that see that far) but, I know I hear God."

There is no doubt that the way -the so-called vulgar talking, intended wall builder not a bridge builder, now President Elect Donald Trump, trumped everyone to emerge in the GOP primaries to win their nomination and eventually the election is full of surprises.

A greater surprise is the way God humbled the CNN projections, sorry media (print and electronic) projections. Prophets predicted the highly experienced 30-year political veteran, humanly favoured, to become the first woman to be in the Oval Office, Hillary Clinton was not able to get there. Another surprise was the self-styled, rhetoric expert, the first Black President-President Barak Obama-in the Oval Office boasted that 'my successor will be a Democrat, my legacies must be protected' saw himself in the saddle of real American politics that stunned him, according to him- making him lick his wounds.

An even greater surprise, is for those Americans and non-Americans who never gave Mr. Donald Trump a chance; including all the living past Presidents of America who refused to endorse him to win the presidency. There are some scriptures that surged to my mind, including the text for this message above and some below:

"But our God is in the heavens: he hath done whatsoever he hath pleased." Psalm 115:3

"Thus saith the LORD to his anointed, to Cyrus, whose right hand I have holden, to subdue nations before him; and I will loose the loins of kings, to open before him the two-leaved gates; and the gates shall not be shut" Isaiah 45:3

Some lessons for you and I:

1. God is interested in the affairs of our nations more than we think and if we can pray he will answer.
2. God is the one that puts people in power, using human elements those willing and unwilling. Dan 2:21-22
3. The nations are like a drop of water in a bucket -Isaiah 40:15
4. With trust and faith in God, hard work, not giving up on yourself, the sky is not your limit. You can achieve your dream. You shall make it! The only person that can write you off, is yourself, not your opponents or, your enemies.

It reminds me of a song in Yoruba:

Ibi ma de, ma de 2ce
Baye ngbo gun b 'Esu n hale
Ibi ma de ma de o laye

(Meaning where I will get to, I will get to, even though the enemy and the world are in opposition I shall fulfill destiny and purpose.) What makes you succeed is not what others do or, do not do but what you do or, do not do. If God has not said it is over, it is not over.

5. God can turn your mess into a message and test into a testimony, as he has done for Donald Trump.

6. For promotion cometh neither from the East, from the West, from the North nor from the South.
God is the judge: 'he putteth down one, and setteth up another.' Psalm 75:6-7 God can do either to you; pray that he put you up not down.

7. It is a matter of time, your enemies are coming with olive branches to beg you to put them in position, as they are begging President - Elect Donald Trump.

8. Pray for Donald Trump, for God to give him wisdom, a heart of forgiveness, capacity and good temperament for rulership; for his sworn enemies not to kill him (protection), to make the right choices, not to abuse the power that God has generously and graciously given to him. To become a David for this generation, not Saul, Ahab or, Hitler!

In conclusion, sit down and think of how you can contribute and benefit from the Presidency of Donald Trump, intellectually, hysically spiritually, materially, ministerially, financially (e.g. you can write a book on him, make a souvenir etc.)

The God who did that for Donald Trump against all odds will do your own.

Be blessed in Jesus name. I'll see you on top.

*Author's note: This piece was written in 2016 November when Donald Trump won the USA election.

Prayer: Lord, by your grace, against human polls and wickedness; take me to the position you have ordained for me.

Quotation: If you don't just want to live an ordinary life, then you will have to be intentional about converting all your time into that which you have been called to do- Unknown.

22

Favour Is For A Purpose

"For if you remain silent at this time, relief and deliverance for the Jews will arise from another place, but you and your father's family will perish. And who knows but that you have come to your royal position for such a time as this?" Esther 4:14 NIV

I am of the school of thought that favour is usually for a purpose. In my book *"Understanding Principles, Purpose, Power, and People of Vision"*, I postulated, that if the purpose of a thing is unknown, abuse is inevitable. Everyone is crying, praying, going to the mountains for favour and I pray God will grant your prayers. But listen to me, favour is for a purpose. Let me give you three scripture references, to buttress my point:

1. *" And the angel came in unto her, and said, Hail, thou that art highly favoured, the Lord is with thee: blessed art thou among women."* Lk 1:28

1. God favoured Mary among women to enable her to bring Jesus to this world, so that the project (purpose) of God to save humanity could be achieved. Let me help you to amplify and apply that to your life. There is a purpose for that pregnancy you are carrying. There is a purpose for that child you have or, you are yet to have. The mother of Thomas Edison may not have had a dramatic angelic visitation like Mary; the mother of The Wesley brothers, the mother of the Wright brothers (who invented the aircraft), the mother of Steve Jobs (who invented the iPad I am using to write this, on which you are probably reading this article) and my mother, your mother were all favoured to bring us to the world to accomplish a purpose. Go ahead and accomplish that purpose. My thesis is that you are on earth and favoured for a purpose, like Mary.

2. *"Now when the turn of Esther, the daughter of Abigail the uncle of Mordecai who had taken her as his daughter, came to go to the king, she did not request anything except what Hegai, the king's eunuch*

who was in charge of the women, advised. And Esther found favour in the eyes of all who saw her." Esther 2:15.

The Bible says Esther was chosen by favour. This orphan, slave, immigrant girl was chosen, why? External beauty, internal beauty, maybe a combination or, none of them, but I know God favoured her and made her queen to save a generation. God usually has a purpose for favouring a person in a dispensation. Mordecai brought this to bear when, the delectable wine and legality of the palace was about to becloud the reasoning of Esther, he said- maybe you are in that palace for a time like this and if you fail to act, God will look for someone else.

Friend, reader, sister, pastor, elder, Deaconess, Bishop, Mr. President, Mr. Prime Minister, Mr. Millionaire, Mr. Billionaire. Mr. Talented, Senator, Congressman, Premier, Governor, Governor General, Minister, General Overseer, you are favoured like Esther to occupy that position. You have a purpose, don't abuse that purpose. Don't use that purpose against God's agenda. Recently, I heard the news in Ontario that the Health Card for citizens will no more show whether the bearer is just a male or female. The driver licenses will now also show 'X' for transgender. During the week, I went to use the toilet at a local College and found out there are toilets labelled as 'gender neutral'. All these are happening in addition to a new very controversial sexual education curriculum introduced in Ontario. My take is that the whole Province is being driven with speed in a particular transgender direction because, the Premier claims to be a Lesbian after having three grown-up children! Whoever you are, you are favoured to occupy your position to serve God's purpose. If you choose to misuse your office like the likes of Pharaoh, Haman and Herod, you will also get the rewards of ending in the Red Sea, being killed on your gallows or waiting for a dirty slap from an invisible angel!

3. Let me give you one more scripture, the controversial scripture: *"For the children being not yet born, neither having done any good or evil, that the purpose of God according to election might stand, not of works, but of him that calleth; 12 It was said unto her, The elder shall*

serve the younger13 As it is written, Jacob have I loved, but Esau have I hated." Rom 9:11-13.

> "I enjoy practicing Jesus Engineering over Chemical Engineering because, I believe I am fulfilling a purpose. Instead of refining oil I am refining human souls. I may not be making millions of dollars but I am affecting million of lives."

I am not God, but I am a child of God, I believe in God, and "I enjoy practicing Jesus Engineering over Chemical Engineering because, I believe I am fulfilling a purpose. Instead of refining oil I am refining human souls. I may not be making millions of dollars but I am affecting million of lives." I asked God the meaning of this scripture, and he made me understand what I am sharing with you; that Jacob was favoured to fulfill the purpose of bringing forth the birth of the nation of Israel. Bring forth a generation that would be a prototype for the coming Church: the body of Christ. For this purpose, Jacob was chosen and preferred above his brother Esau. Time will fail me to elucidate, on more biblical men and women of God that were favoured in the Bible but, all without exemption was for a purpose; people like Ruth, Rahab, Deborah, Noah, Abraham, Moses, Joshua, Joseph, John the Baptist, Peter and Paul, even Jesus. Lk 2.52 says he had favour with man and God. That is why at Gethsemane, he said 'not my will but God's'. When you pray for favour to secure a job, you are not going to that office to sleep. When you pray to secure favour to become a mother, trust me, be ready to raise those children in a godly way.

This is your month of favour but, as you ask for favour be ready to fill the corresponding responsibility that favour bestows. Don't waste or abuse favour. Fulfill the purpose of favour and let favour fulfill its purpose in your life. May you fulfill a purpose in Jesus name. Jesus is Lord!

Prayer: O' Lord Favour me. You favoured Samuel, John The Baptist and Jesus Christ. Favour me in life.

Quotation: *"The favour of God, forfeits the failure of men."* -**Gift Gugu Mona**

23

Gather Against The Gatherers So That You Can Gather Their Spoils.

"It came to pass after this also, that the children of Moab, and the children of Ammon, and with them other beside the Ammonites, came against Jehoshaphat to battle." 2 Chronicles 20:1

The children of Moab. The children of Ammon. The other children, nameless.

What that tells me is that most times we make noise about the enemies we know. What of those we do not know?

Who are the gatherers? Essentially: Moabites and Ammonites.

Let me give you four categories of gatherers against you today, according to that scripture:

1. Biblically speaking Moabites and Ammonites, they are the descendants of Lot that separated from Abraham. Lot had two daughters. The two daughters slept incestuously with their father to produce Moabites and Ammonites. (Genesis 19:37-38). The older daughter had a son named Moab ("from father"), and the younger gave birth to Ben-Ammi ("son of my people"). The Ammonites, descendants of Ben-Ammi, were a nomadic people who lived in the territory of modern-day Jordan. The name of the capital city, Amman, reflects the name of those ancient inhabitants. They are part of the Arab nation today.

   Who are the gathers? They are the enemies of the gospel today. They call themselves radical Islam. They formed ISIS, Boko Haram, Al Shabaab, The Hezbollah, The Muslim Brotherhood, Al- Qaeda, and other terrorist groups. They kill and maim in the name of religion.

2. They are the LGBT group who are re-defining the Bible, particularly in the area of marriage. They are the rich and powerful, who have invaded the highest office of governance, particularly in the Western world. They go by the name PRIDE.

   They are the ones, that have made it possible for prayers, biblical and moral principles to be alien in the schools. They have invaded churches even the Vatican is not spared.

   Who are the gatherers?

3. They are satanic agents in their hierarchy:

   "For we wrestle not against flesh and blood, but against principalities, against powers, against the rulers of the darkness of this world, against spiritual wickedness in high places." They are invisible forces.

   Who are the gatherers?

4. They are the usual challenges we face in our daily lives: barrenness, sicknesses & disease, joblessness, ministerial challenges, financial trap, debt, poverty, spiritual dryness, afflictions, attacks of all dimensions, bad dreams, business failure, academic failure, health challenges. These are the Ammonites and Moabites challenging your Jehoshaphat.

THEIR FOCUS.

Their focus is to take Jehoshaphat and the job will be done. The enemies gather against Jehoshaphat, the King, the representative of Israel. Against Israel, Judah and Jerusalem. Meaning they gather against the Church and the Church leadership: the pastors, the ministers, the evangelists; they do not permit open air crusades anymore. They are against Christians and all they represent; our children, our future. They gather against the Western World, America, Canada, United Kingdom, and The European Union. These are nations that spread the gospel across the world but today are busy spreading 'another gospel' they call it "New World Order."

THEIR STRATEGY.

Do you notice that Ministers are afraid, to preach the undiluted Word of God now. Apart from those preaching extreme prosperity and grace message; even those who want to preach a 'balanced message' are afraid of being called 'homophobic'. Basically, every message that is not politically correct is termed 'hate speech.' God help us. God loves sinners and hates sin, so should his ambassadors on earth.

The devil is a strategist and economist. Let me explain. The Bible says 'take the shepherd and the sheep will scatter.' Matt 26:31 Many pastors in our time, are wondering why the battle is fierce against their ministry.

Many fathers and husbands, are wondering why the battle is fierce against their household and marriages.

Many presidents, prime ministers, heads of governments particularly who are children of God are wondering why the battle is so fierce against them. The reason is simple; to take the shepherd so the sheep will be scattered.

About 30 years ago, I read a book called 'The Strategy of Satan' by Warren Wiersbe. The author exposes the ways the devil strategizes with his limited angels. You recall that Satan was the morning star. Being full of pride and with a sizeable number of angels, he staged a coup against God in heaven. The result, these angels were now turned to devils or, demonic spirits. These demons are not as many as humans.

Now, when Satan goes to a church, let's say the numbers of members are 1000. He will need at least 1000 demons, to ensure that the word of God preached by the pastor does not have an effect on anyone. Lk 8:5 says the sower went to sow and some fell by the waysides, and had no chance of growing because, 'the birds of the air' picked them up! Jesus says the bird of the air is Satan. There is only one Satan, so, it means Satan will have to go from one person to another-he doesn't have that luxury. So, rather than send a thousand demons to a church of 1000, he will rather send 10-50 demons against the pastor or, preacher to ensure that he does not preach the right word. In essence, he will gather against the preachers and scatter the preachers.

That explains why the messages you are hearing today may be 'another gospel', apology to Brother Paul.

Many years ago, in my university days around 1980, my Pastor, Professor A. M. A. Imevbore was invited by late Archbishop Benson

Idahosa from Ile - Ife to Benin. I was the one that drove my pastor and few of us. It was one of Idahosa's conventions and there was a large crowd. As my pastor was preaching the Lord opened my eyes and I saw some people like demons throwing arrows at him! I quickly called other team members, that our job was not to listen to the message but, to intercede. So, we gathered in another room and began praying for our pastor.

If anyone does attack you, it will not be my doing; whoever attacks you will surrender to you. Isaiah 54:15

Jehoshaphat gathered all the gatherable: Starting with God, The Priests, The choir, The Levites, the Kohathites, and Korhites, The instrumentalists, The prayer warriors, The intercessors, The chorus leaders, The prophet (Jahaziel), The psalmists (sons of Asaph),The wives, children, and the congregation:

"3. *And Jehoshaphat feared, and set himself to seek the LORD, and proclaimed a fast throughout all Judah. 4. And Judah gathered them together, to ask help of the LORD: even out of all the cities of Judah they came to* seek the LORD 13. *And all Judah stood before the LORD, with their little ones, their wives, and their children.*

19. And the Levites, of the Children of Kohathies and of the children of the Korhities, stood up to praise the LORD God of Isreal with a loud voice on high." 2 Chrons. 20:3-19 KJV

And guess what?! When they gathered and sang, God set Jehosaphat and the people free and they in turn gathered the spoils of the people. When the enemy gathers against you, gather the people of God and confront the enemy, through singing and praying, fasting and I guarantee you, you will gather the spoil of the enemy.

"And when Jehoshaphat and his people came to take away the spoil of them, they found among them in abundance both riches with the dead bodies, and precious jewels, which they stripped off for themselves, more than they could carry away: and they were three days in gathering of the spoil, it was so much" Ch 20:25

> "All you need to do is gather against the gatherers and you shall gather their spoils!"

Don't be afraid of people gathering against you don't ignore them either. "All you need to do is gather against the gatherers and you shall gather their spoils!"

Prayer: No matter who gathers against me help me to gather against the enemy and give me their spoils.

Quotation: *"To gather with God's people in united adoration of the Father is as necessary to the Christian life as prayer."* **-Martin Luther**

24

The Processes(stages) of Divine Intervention

"So I prophesied as he commanded me, and the breath came into them, and they lived, and stood up upon their feet, an exceeding great army." Ezekiel 37:10.

The dry bones story of Ezekiel, shows how God intervenes in the affairs of men stage-wise, when we do what is mandatory. For every promise of God, there is a condition. There are simple requirements from you by God, for him to intervene in your situation. Even if it is too difficult for you, to see what he can do because of the seeming hopelessness (dryness of the bones). He demands that you prophesy(pray) and you continue to do it consistently.

I saw four stages I want to share:

1. Scattered bones stage
2. Skeleton stage
3. Corpse Stage
4. Living stage

Scattered Bones Stage:

We all in life face the scattered bones stage. We are totally confused, no career, no prospect, no money, no parents, no helper. Then, we begin to pray and before we know it helpers come and we are able to go to school or start a business. Prophesy to the wind, God commands and we do. We finish school. Now we need a job. Prophesy son of man. We get a job. Now we need a life partner. Prophesy again. Life partner comes. Now we need children. Prophesy the voice says, you prophesied as commanded-it takes a while-but, before you know it, you and your spouse have raised an army of children - your quiver is full. Psalm 127.

Skeleton stage:

Another scenario is, you have graduated but you are jobless, it is your dry bones stage. So you want to change your location or, relocate to another country. You begin to prophesy 'visa', Visa comes for you to land overseas. You are a walking skeleton.

Corpse Stage:

You need money to make the trip. As you pray, you find money to travel abroad. You literally become a corpse on arrival. No seeming future. No career. No job, no car. Bad credit or, no credit. No house, rented house or, community house. Maybe you are even seeking asylum living in a shelter, the situation looks dead. The voice comes, your pastor admonishes pray, don't give up, and prophesy. Your situation changes.

Living stage:

I remember, when we came to Canada and with the money we brought we were buying this and buying that. I began to prophesy 'Canada you will vomit this money'. Trust me, I am still prophesying and by the divine intervention of God family-wise ministry-wise, I see us raising an army. An army of anointed children biologically and spiritually.

I don't know the stage you are in but, take a cue from above; prophesy. Start prophesying to that scattered bones situation. What you call a bad situation is really a progressive situation. Where you are today is better than where you were yesteryear.

Ezekiel kept prophesying, from dry bone, to skeleton, the skeleton stage was still scary but it was better than the scattered bones. He prophesied and skeletons became corpses, nobody wants to see a dead person, but guess what a corpse in this case was a greater blessing and level than a skeleton. Then he prophesied and the corpses arose and became an army. Wow. Life is lived in stages. I used to know a photographer from Ado-Ekiti he calls himself 'Little by Little.' Through photography he has not only become a millionaire but was recognised by the Federal Government and given The Commander of Nigeria CON. Keep serving God, keep reading and meditating on the Word; keep running away from sin, keep being faithful to God and your spouse, keep training your children in the way of thy Lord; keep praying, keep trusting God to improve your finances as you keep being generous to God and humanity. It is a function of time, you will be prosperous. Not only that, you will raise disciples, prosperous people, you shall raise an eagle generation. A people that will turn our world around for the better. The world is waiting for you to manifest. You shall! Rom 8:18-19. I see your dry bones situation becoming an army of joyful men and women in the Lord. You are not a chicken you are an eagle, you shall live and not die.

Prayer: No matter how confused, depressed or, sick I am You have demonstrated that prayer and confession turns situations around. Therefore, I prophesy to the dry bones of my life, dry bones live again. Whatever is dead and looks impossible to turn around, hear the Word of God, "Live!" Through the word of God I create a new status for my life.

Quotation: *"The Word of God spoke into the dry bones. His breath filled them, put tendons and put skin on...Then you will know I am God...When Jesus comes that will happen."* -**Louie Giglio**

25

Let The Children Come To Jesus

"But Jesus said, "Let the children come to me. Don't stop them! For the Kingdom of Heaven belongs to those who are like these children." 15 And he placed his hands on their heads and blessed them before he left." Mark 10:16

Three things happened in this passage. First, Jesus rebuked those who are preventing children from coming to Him. Secondly, he taught us another kingdom principle, "for the kingdom of heaven belongs to those who are like these children" and thirdly, he laid hands on them and blessed them.

God has told us to avoid distractions. My question to you today is, what are you doing to distract/prevent children, youth, adults from coming to the Master- the Lord Jesus Christ?

Let us look at the first thing, some get to positions of authority, and change moral biblical principles to immoral principles. They remove anything about God, prayers and biblical principles from public schools and the political arena. Some tell you, they have 'evolved' in their thinking and so, they permit and use their position to encourage ungodly gender lifestyles. Some in their positions misappropriate funds meant to feed children; funds meant to give them proper education. Funds meant to build hospitals, take care of orphans, are used to buy exotic cars and private jets. Funds meant to take care of refugees and internationally displaced children and to rescue kidnapped children are used to build sprawling mansions. Some hide money in bunkers, and tankers and use this money to prevent justice. What are you doing to offend God and humanity?

Stories abound of incest and sexual abuse, raping of minors and human trafficking not just in small villages, but on a global level. What are you doing to hurt children and their future? Mothers, what training are you giving your children by your ungodly lifestyles? I see mothers who are into prostitution. I see fathers raping their children. I see mothers and fathers in our time not just watching pornography but engaging in making pornography. Haba!

I see many parents who are tattoo crazy. Some spiritualize tattoo by making godly signs on their bodies. It is like stealing and bringing the money to church, you are still doing a wrong thing! I see many who are drunkards. I see many who live on proceeds of corruption and consequent curses and use such money to send those children to expensive schools; lavish them with expensive cars and wanton luxury living. I see parents 'helping' their children to cheat in exams to secure admission or secure jobs. What are you doing to prevent children from coming to Jesus?

We are in an age, particularly in Canada and the Western world where we are too busy, we have no time to take children to Sunday School or, to attend church services. We have time however, to take them to all manner of sporting events and weekend parties, but no time to introduce them to the Lord Jesus at a tender age.

Do you know, you are preventing children from coming to the Master when you abuse them, physically leaving them with broken bones and bruises? Do you know that ignoring children's needs, putting them in unsupervised, dangerous situations or, making children feel worthless or, stupid is also child abuse? This is emotional abuse of children.

Friend, Jesus warns you! Stop it. Stop abusing children. Stop preventing them from learning about Me(Jesus). Stop preventing them from learning about virtue because, nature has no vacuum. When they are not learning virtue they are learning vices.

Before you think Pastor Dada is writing about sinners or, to unbelievers, let me remind you that Jesus was talking to his disciples; in our own time, Christians!

The second thing Jesus focused on, was that the Kingdom belongs to those who are childlike in faith. Children are inquisitive, they do not want only to learn, they learn quickly. Take time to teach them virtue. Prepare them for a godly lifestyle in the future, to be a better spouse, a better citizen, a better politician, a better professor, governor, president, school, teacher, administrator. Prepare them to be good leaders. Teach them principles, that will help boys become men that treat ladies and their wives with dignity and respect. Teach them, so that girls become mothers to be genuine home keepers and home builders. We are tired of frivolous and baseless divorces. If you care to know, divorce has more impact on children than you can imagine. The man or, the woman can go and remarry, but leave the children to parental imbalance and step parents who are steps to nothing but abuse.

What is the point of all the time, energy and resources you spend on your children and they grow up not knowing God?

The third thing, Jesus laid hands on them and blessed them. You want these children to prosper? Let Jesus supervise them. Let him guide them through his word. Let him lay hands on them. Jesus laying hands on the children is about the transfer of power, anointing, and virtue. This he wants to do through you as parents.

We shall see our children on top!

Prayer: O' Lord help me to raise my children in a godly way. Make me a good and godly parent. Help me to bring them to Jesus and not take them away from Jesus.

Quotation: *"Train up a child in the way he should go; even when he is old he will not depart from it."* -**King Solomon**

26

What Are You Experiencing, A Lifting Up Or A Bringing Down

"The LORD maketh poor, and maketh rich: he bringeth low, and lifteth up." 1 Samuel 2:7-8

Hannah can say that again! She has experienced a lifting up. But wait a minute because God has power to make poor and power to make rich, because he has power to bring low and lift up does that mean you have no input in the process?

In Genesis 1 in the creation process God was sovereign. He kept declaring - let there be light, let the waters separate, let the earth bring forth and it was so. But he did not use those sovereignty influences to make man. He consulted the Trinity. Then they designed man. Then he breathed into man. That made the difference. Others were inanimate. Yes, animals, fish are not completely inanimate but they were in the phylum of 'let there be' category. Even though they are alive they are not in the same category with man. That is not where we are going today. Today is about lifting up and bringing down. The point is God made man in a special class influencing their destiny. He gave them power to make choices. That makes the difference. ((**Your lifting up or coming down is not entirely God's decision you are part of the equation.**))Believe it or not, the first man he made was Adam. He gave him an assignment to name animals. He scored A+. Then God decided to help him, by giving him a helpmate to enjoy life - recreate and procreate. Then bang Adam could not manage Eve. Scored F-. Before you could say Jack Robinson, they were down from their lifted position. They lost their estate and became vagabonds. They experienced a bringing down.

Fast forward to the time Hannah had to decide her future. Hannah was one of the two wives of Elkanah. We are not sure who was the first and who was the second. It really did not matter there were heavier matters to contend with.

We read: "But unto Hannah he gave a worthy portion; for he loved Hannah: but the LORD had shut up her womb. And her adversary also provoked her sore, for to make her fret, because the LORD had shut up her womb' 1 Sam 1 : 5-6. Bang, Hannah was on the wrong side of a heavenly decision - The Lord had shut her womb! When a big problem has brought you down, small ones have greater chances of messing you up. The second wife began to provoke her- "and her adversaries provoked her sore" meaning -brought her lower than low! Have you experienced that before! Most likely!

But that is not the end of the story. Hannah knew only God can repair her situation. She began to sing. 'God lifts up and brings down' was her first composed but unreleased album. God has the power to lift her up, but she needed to make an input not just to change the trajectory of her life but to accelerate the process. Her concern was how? What can you do to experience a lifting up?

First, **she was going to Shiloh faithfully**. Do you serve God faithfully? Do you go to church regularly? How are you serving God? Or are you a weather dependent kind of church goer?

Secondly, **she developed her prayer power,** was tired of begging Eli for prayer- no mean intention. Are you still seeking for prayer contractors before you can get anything done in your life? Imagine if Hannah had depended on Eli for a vision?

Thirdly, **she became creative**. She went beyond the norm. What will I do to make God change my situation? Let me make a vow, and that was the game changer. I am yet to know why vow making triggers God for lifting up people. Serving God is neither dogmatic, dull or faceless. Think of what you can do to make God happy after all you were created for his pleasure. Revelations 4:11. Think of what you can do to make your pastor happy. Eli's lack of proper diagnosis or better still, discerning of Hannah's case was enough weapon for Hannah to leave that church. But she was on a journey, a journey of destiny change. She was too Eagle eyed to focus on being chicken hearted. Notice that she completely ignored her mate provoking her too. Silence is the best answer for a fool!

Fast forward again, after one year her story had changed, the barren had become the mother. The provoked had become a gospel artist that has her album lyrics in the scripture. Obliviously topping all the radio, iTunes, and all music promotional charts of her time. The woman that was a reproach in the society has become a celebrity of a sort. The same God that shut her womb had opened her womb. She has experienced a lifting up.

That shall be your portion in Jesus name! Notice that the ones provoking her had suffered a major set back, I almost said heart attack, she had gone down she had been brought down. That will not be your portion. None of Peninnah's children were named in scripture not to talk of having two books (1 & 2 Samuel) named after her son, like Hannah.

What the Holy Spirit taught me today is that The way you treat your neighbour, husband, Pastor, church member, co-worker, the way you pray, and give will be factored into your lifting up or coming down. the way you live your life, the way you manage your situation, the way you handle simple or complex situations, the way you serve God or otherwise will be a major factor in deciding whether you will be brought down or lifted up. As they say, 'qui cera cera' or "what will be will be" has no place in the bible. You can decide, God will be the one to do the lifting up or bringing down but you will be the one to produce what God will use to bring you down or lift you up! After all if God has put water in a well, it is your duty to find rope and bucket to fetch it. Otherwise don't blame God for your starvation. The angel only helped Hagar to locate the well!

It is our year of flourishing - go and do the work that will make you to flourish. Go and pray the prayers. Go and make the vows. And don't forget to wean Samuel (produce and products) and bring him back to God. Shalom.

Prayer: O Lord help me to do what I need to do to experience a lifting up in Jesus' name.

Quotation: *"Walk with the dreamers, the believers, the courageous, the cheerful, the planners, the doers, the successful people with their heads in the clouds and their feet on the ground. Let their spirit light a fire within you to leave this world better than when you found it."* – **Wilfred Peterson**

27

Avoid Sexual Immorality

"Now regarding the questions you asked in your letter. Yes, it is good to abstain from sexual relations. 2 But because there is so much sexual immorality, each man should have his own wife, and each woman should have her own husband" 1 Cor 7:1-2.

"Worldly desires, appetites, and feelings prevent true Christianity. The human will is, in a sense, enslaved by fleshly and worldly desires. It is therefore necessary, for God to awaken people to a sense of guilt and danger and thus produce an opposite excitement or feeling and desire. This counter-feeling breaks the power of worldly desire and leaves the will free to obey God."

-Charles G. Finney

"Excessive sexual sin and nakedness is one of the marks of our Western culture and much of the world today. Everything is sensual. Everything must be sexy. We live in a sex-crazed world, and nakedness jumps out at us from everywhere. It is becoming more and more difficult for men and women to keep themselves in a state of moral purity."

-Bert Farias

Listen to me my friend, God is not just a God of purpose, He is the God of order. In His purposeful agenda, He made man male and female. "God wired into human nature sexual components that will make sex within them easy and be able to achieve the three major purposes for marriage and sexual activities: companionship, recreation, and procreation." Then he gave them boundaries and guidelines to enjoy this relationship.

Here are some of them:

1. Avoid Homosexuality
   "Do not practice homosexuality, having sex with another man as with a woman. It is a detestable sin." Lev 18:22 NLT
   Avoid male to male, female to female sexual relationships. Sexual activity must be between man and woman only.

   > "God wired into human nature sexual components that will make sex within them easy and be able to achieve the three major purposes for marriage and sexual activities: companionship, recreation, and procreation."

   "For this cause God gave them up unto vile affections: for even their women did change the natural use into that which is against nature: 27 And likewise also the men, leaving the natural use of the woman, burned in their lust one toward another; men with men working that which is unseemly, and receiving in themselves that recompense of their error which was meet." Rom 1:26-27

2. Avoid prostitution
   "Do you not know that he who unites himself with a prostitute is one with her in body? For it is said, "The two will become one flesh."" 1 Cor 6:16 NIV

3. Avoid pre-marital sex-known as fornication.
   "....Now the body is not for fornication, but for the Lord; and the Lord for the body" 1 Cor 6:13 KJV

4. Avoid incest.

"*Do not have sexual relations with your sister, either your father's daughter or your mother's daughter, whether she was born in the same home or elsewhere.*" Lev 18:9; 10-18

5. Avoid Bestiality.

"*Do not have sexual relations with an animal and defile yourself with it. A woman must not present herself to an animal to have sexual relations with it; that is a perversion.*" Lev 18:23

6. Get married. Stay with your spouse.

"*Therefore shall a man leave his father and his mother, and shall cleave unto his wife: and they shall be one flesh.*"
Gen 2:24, 1 Cor 7:1-2

7. Avoid Adultery. Once you are married, you get stuck with your spouse forever.

"*Do not have sexual relations with your neighbor's wife and defile yourself with her.*" Lev 18:20.

8. Avoid Divorce, separation, and remarriage.

No divorce. No separation, no remarriage unless death separates you. Matt 19:3-10

9. Don't watch pornography or, related newly invented audio, virtual sexual perversions.

"*Now the works of the flesh are manifest, which are these; Adultery, fornication, uncleanness, lasciviousness, 20 Idolatry, witchcraft, hatred, variance, emulations, wrath, strife, seditions, heresies, 21 Envyings, murders, drunkenness, revellings, and such like: of the which I tell you before, as I have also told you in time past, that they which do 'such things 'shall not inherit the kingdom of God.*" Gal 5:19-21 KJV
A modern day invention of sexual immorality is under the phrase "such things"; including those ones that are yet to be invented! For example, watching of pornography, electronic or, in print, movies, listening to erotic songs, will add no value to your spiritual growth.

10. Avoid Tattoos. "Do not cut your bodies for the dead or put tattoo marks on yourselves. I am the LORD" (Leviticus 19:28).

11. Avoid Lewdness: unashamed indecency, unbridled lust, unrestrained depravity, provocativeness, seductiveness, temptatiousness, seditious dressing and nudity. "Now the body is not for sexual immorality

but for the Lord, and the Lord for the body. And God both raised up the Lord and will also raise us up by His power" (1 Cor. 6:13-14).

Conclusion: As I conclude this piece, take this counsel and warning from the Hebrew author.

"Marriage is honourable in all, and the bed undefiled: but whoremongers and adulterers God will judge." Heb 13:4.

Take the cure. Paul says "Get married" if you cannot "abstain." God favoured you, to give you your vital organs for a legitimate purpose because, favour is for a purpose. Do not abuse God's grace in your life. If you are married, be content with your spouse. If you are not married, wait till you get married and honour your body.

Lastly, remember going against these guidelines exposes you to dangerous, spiritual, physical, medical, social and even legal consequences. Half a word is for the wise.

"Do you not know that your bodies are members of Christ? Shall I then take the members of Christ and make them members of a harlot? Certainly not! Or, do you not know that your body is the temple of the Holy Spirit who is in you, whom you have from God, and you are not your own? For you were bought at a price; therefore glorify God in your body and in your spirit, which are God's" (1 Cor. 6:15, 19-20)

Prayer: Deliver me O' Lord from lustful desires.

Quotation 1: *"That you abstain from things offered to idols, from blood, from things strangled, and sexual immorality. If you keep yourselves, from these you do well. Farewell"* -Acts 15:29 **The Council of Elders in Jerusalem.**

Quotation 2: *"Regardless of what society says, we can't go on much longer in the sea of immorality without judgment coming."* - **Billy Graham**

28

Don't Forget Your Destiny Helpers

"And when they came to Reuel their father, he said, How is it that ye are come so soon to day?

19 And they said, An Egyptian delivered us out of the hand of the shepherds, and also drew water enough for us, and watered the flock. 20 And he said unto his daughters, And where is he? Why is it that ye have left the man? call him, that he may eat bread." Ex 2:18-20

I was reading a book a Pastor friend gave me tilted:"Making the Most of Every Opportunity." Written by Pastor Moses Adedipe. One of the chapters is the topic of our devotional this morning. The butler forgot Joseph in prison. It is so easy to forget helpers. The Yorubas have an adage for virtually everything. One of them relevant to our discussion is "Eni to yagbe le gbagbe eni to ko ko le gbagbe". In those days there were no water closet toilets as we see today. People would defecate anyhow and in some cases, some people have to pack the faeces. Hence the proverb. 'the person who for convenience easily defecate could easily forget but not the one that packed it to clean up the mess.'

Adedipe said "You became or got there because God placed some people to help you get to the top. Many of us do not remember the name of our teachers in college, not to mention high school."

How easy it is for you to forget those who have been a blessing in your life. Many of us only see the mistakes of our helpers, we never think about their inconveniences and their sacrifices. We quickly forget them, reject them and abuse them.

Think a while how we treat our pastors. In the time of trouble we call, he will go the extra mile to see us out of trouble. The moment we are comfortable, we shake our buttocks and like butterflies, we fly away.

I can give you many examples but, this is one that really touched me. I had a very unpleasant experience with a young man about 12 years ago. He came to church and he was a student in one of the local universities. He was baptized in the church. He had a challenge one time and I held 21 days night vigil with this young man. I remember giving him my car a Toyota Camry as a gift.

Then he disappeared for some years. He called me from a distant country asking for his baptismal certificate. I could not get it to him because of the bureaucracy of our Mission. Then, he got married and all he told everybody that cares to listen including his wife about me was that I said I did not know him! He went everywhere he could and defamed me and slandered me. Have you been there before? Why do we take time to do evil to those who have done us good? When people are doing you good, most times they do it to fulfill God's purpose in their life.

Of course, it is not possible to remember all the people that have done you good, but that is not the point. The point is make a conscious effort to remember your destiny helpers and repay them with good rewards. Some are even dead, but they have relations. Remember how Saul hated David, but Jonathan loved him? One day David remembered Jonathans son Mephibosheth. And brought him to live in the Kings palace and eat on his table. Someone helped you to succeed; help others to succeed.

Prayer: O' Lord help me to remember my helpers and reward them wonderfully. O' Lord let those I have helped remember me and do me good. O Lord, in the words of Nehemiah, remember me for good.

Quotation: *"When you have no helpers, see your helpers in God. When you have many helpers, see God in all your helpers. When you have nothing but God, see all in God. When you have everything, see God in everything. Under all conditions, stay thy heart only on the Lord."* - **Charles Spurgeon**

29

Thou Shall Be Favoured

"By this I know that thou favourest me, because my mine enemy doth not triumph over me." Psalm 41:11 [KJV]

♦ Favour is manifestation without the hand of flesh.
♦ Favour is when everything is working for you.
♦ Favour is when those who hate you turn around to love you.
♦ Favour is getting what you did not ask for and not missing the one you requested.
♦ Favour is when you do your shopping and heaven pays the bill.
♦ Favour is what commands attention to you.
♦ Favour makes you to be a source of wonder.
♦ Favour is when everything you touch prospers.
♦ Favour is when you forget your past failure because, the blessings have multiplied.
♦ Favour is when you receive an act of kindness beyond what is due or, usual.
♦ Favour is when someone or, a group of people show approval for you or prefer you above others.
♦ Favour is when men everywhere you go shower you with blessing.
♦ Favour is when everything you touch turns to gold.
♦ Favour is when heaven smiles at you.
♦ Favour is experiencing triumph where your mates are struggling
♦ Favour is better than labour!
♦ "Favour is grace. God's prerogative"

Prayer: In 1 Sam 2:26 Samuel was favoured by God and men. In Lk 1:80 John The Baptist was favoured by God and men. In Lk 5:52 Jesus was favoured by God and men. From

> "Favour is grace. God's prerogative"

today let Amos Dele Dada(put your name here) be highly favoured by God and men.

Quotation: *"You must work for grace and favor to work for you."*
  -Unkown

30

Check List For Victorious Living Or Overcoming Life Challenges.

"For whatsoever is born of God overcometh the world: and this is the victory that overcometh the world, even our faith."
1 John 5:4

Before you submit your application for a visa, when applying to enter a country, the country always requests you bring some documents to see if you qualify for admittance to their nation.

The final phase of your preparation is, 'going through this checklist before submission' if you want your application to be considered at all. Non-compliance with the checklist shows you are not ready to have your visa approved.

The Christian life has a checklist for victorious life on earth and also for getting a visa for the rapture. I have compiled fifty of such qualifying items; I will dole them out in tens starting from now. They are in bullet points, lets go:

Develop your relationship with God.

1. You must be born again John 3:3-8; 2Cor 5:17. Your life must be rearranged not refurbished.
   Those who are born again do not commit adultery. No hot temper.
2. You must have a divine encounter. Every man that did exploits in the Bible had an encounter:
   Moses, Elisha, Elijah, Jeremiah, and Isaiah.
3. You must die to yourself. Meaning that your flesh must die.
4. You must be filled with the Holy Ghost. Acts 4:1-2 Be filled every day. The key to supernatural power is the Holy
   Ghost. There is no man on earth, that can have victory over sin without the power of God.
5. Key into the attitude of prayer. The more you pray the more power you have.
   No prayer, no power. If there is a man to pray there is a God to answer.
6. Key into the Word of God. Know the Bible. Read the Bible daily. Study it. Memorize it. Understand it. Digest it. Be an addict of the word of God. More than anything apply it to your life.
7. Engage yourself in purposeful deliberate fasting. Jesus said, "But this kind does not go out except by prayer and fasting." Matthew 17:21
8. Meditate on the Word. Reading is like scanning through. Studying helps you to comprehend while meditation delivers the content to you.
9. Develop great spiritual thirst and hunger for the things of God. Blessed are those who hunger and thirst for righteousness, for they shall be satisfied. Matthew 5; 6
10. Become a broken Christian. Broken Christians obey God. Many Christians make Jesus Saviour but, not Lord, not prepared to do his will. Many Christians are out to 'use Jesus'. I am sorry for you; you cannot use Jesus and dump him. He has the final say.

New set. Live a Godly Life Style.

1. There is a dangerous three letter word called SIN. Success In Nothing. It has ruined countless lives starting from Adam and

Eve. Purpose in your heart that whatever it will take, it will not rule and ruin your life.

2. Have a deep love for God. Be the first one to come out when they want to do anything for God. Be available for God.
3. Consistently pursue and live a life of personal integrity; integrity does not mean you are perfect, but you are on track. More than anything, you are who you are anywhere; no two faces, no hypocrisy.
4. Pursue holiness. Without holiness no man shall see the Lord.
5. Have a consistent regular effective prayer life.
6. Be sure that godly character through the fruits of the spirit manifests in your life.

> "Don't just give up in your life without a fight."

7. Practice genuine humility.
8. Persevere. There will always be roadblocks and oppositions when you want to do a great thing. "Don't just give up in your life without a fight."
9. Cultivate the habit of coming to the house of God regularly and punctually. Those who come early are blessed with early Angels.
10. Be teachable. Be a learner. The day you stop learning you start dying.

Change your approach to life. Live more Spiritually.

1. Live your life by faith, not by sight.
2. Practice brokenness. Live soberly not ostentatiously.
3. Be generous. Don't be in the camp of those who give God tips. Who treat God like a beggar. Those who have millions of dollars in the bank and refuse to appreciate God with their gifts and talents. Be an Abel not a Cain
4. Work hard. Most times 'A' students are students that work hard.
5. Be a good time manager. Manage your time well. You cannot recycle time.
6. Be confident in the Lord. Put your trust in the Lord. Like the three Hebrew boys.
7. Practice loyalty. Whether it is comfortable or not. Be loyal. Be committed to a cause.

8. Be disciplined. Discipline your mouth. Discipline your temper. Discipline your appetite. Discipline your body. Discipline your life.

9. Have self-control. Paul says I control myself so that after preaching the gospel I will not be a castaway. Examine yourself.

10. Practice honesty and integrity. Avoid deceit.

Seek Jesus through challenges.

> "Imbibe the spirit of patience. Graduate to long suffering where necessary"

1. Whenever you are faced with a situation, ask yourself what would Jesus do before taking action.

2. Live within your means. Cut your coat according to your cloth, not according to your length.

3. Be a tither and a giver to God.

4. Stop procrastination. Spiritual procrastination after some time I will attend bible study, I will attend prayer meeting, after some time I will read through the Bible. Later, I will go to school. Go now!

5. Always live your life with eternity in view. Time here is short. Eternity is endless.

6. Be filled with the Holy Ghost. Desire the Holy Spirit.

7. Identify your weaknesses and correct them.

8. Always seek and ask for God's wisdom in all you are doing.

9. "Imbibe the spirit of patience. Graduate to long suffering where necessary"

10. Be quick to apologize when you are wrong.

You can key into your overcoming power.

1. Don't be a copycat. You are original.

2. Be a leader not just a manager. The manager maintains; a leader innovates.

> "Don't take God for granted. So that you will not be grounded"

3. Avoid foolish unprofitable company.

4. Purpose to serve God in your generation.

5. Start your day with prayer. Read Psalm 91 read the word. Don't go out in a day without prayer. When you

return thank God for giving you victory for that day. "Don't take God for granted. So that you will not be grounded"

6. Trust God to bring you out of any challenge.
7. Through being hospitable.
8. Learn to forgive and forget.
9. Purpose to leave a good legacy in life. Plan to leave a mark, a positive footprint.
10. Tell yourself I will fulfill destiny on earth and I will make heaven at all cost.

Prayer: I am tired of defeat either in some areas or on a general scale. Oh Lord give me uncommon victory in all areas of my life.

Quotation: *"Victory belongs to the most persevering."* -**Napoleon Bonaparte**

31

Seven Sources Of Power In The Scriptures

There are seven locations of power in the Bible. You must do your best to receive power for victory from them.

1. Power in the Word of God.   *Heb 4:12*

2. Power in the Gospel.   *Romans 1:16*

3. Power in Prayer.   *1Thes 5:17*

4. Power in the Blood of Jesus.   *Rev 12: 11*

5. Power of The Holy Ghost.   *Act 1:8*

6. The Resurrection Power.   *Phil 3:10*

7. Power in the Name of Jesus.   *John 14:14*

Prayer: Pray that you will be saturated with the power of God. Power of God makes the difference. Pray that the Holy Ghost will never leave you.

Quotation : "The Spirit-filled life is not a special, deluxe edition of Christianity. It is part and parcel of the total plan of God for His people." **A. W. Tozer**

32

Focus So That You Can Finish Well:

Case study of Billy Graham, Chuck Templeton & Bron Clifford

"Not as though I had already attained, either were already perfect: but I follow after, if that I may apprehend that for which also I am apprehended of Christ Jesus. Brethren, I count not myself to have apprehended: but this one thing I do, forgetting those things which are behind, and reaching forth unto those things which are before" Phil 3:12-13

I have read the above scripture several times, and I have always allowed it to guide me in the face of challenges, discouragement, rejection, embarrassment, hardship, loneliness, persecution and trials that I have faced in my ministry over the past 31 years.

This is our month of favour but, you will need to continue your focus on Christ to make it to the finish line. Read and learn from this story by Steve Farrar:

"Just about everybody has heard of Billy Graham, but what about

Chuck Templeton? What about Bron Clifford? Have you ever heard of them? Did you know that they were also packing our auditoriums in 1945 when Billy Graham first preached to large crowds? I want to share with you some thoughts prompted by Pastor Tommy Barnett of Phoenix. All three of these young men rose to prominence, in their mid-twenties. One seminary president, after hearing Chuck Templeton – a brilliant, dynamic preacher – called him the most gifted, talented young preacher in America. Templeton and Graham became very close friends. They started preaching together with the Youth For Christ organization. Most observers thought that Templeton would be the one who would go to the top. One magazine wrote a feature article calling Templeton the "Babe Ruth of evangelism."

Bron Clifford was another gifted, young fireball evangelist. Many believed that Clifford was the most gifted powerful preacher to come up in the church for many centuries. People lined up for hours to hear him preach. When he went to Baylor University to give a discourse, they actually cut the ropes off the bells of the tower. They wanted nothing to interfere with his preaching. For two and one half-hours the students of Baylor sat on the edges of their seats as he gave a dissertation on "Christ and the Philosopher's Stone." At age 25, Clifford touched more lives, influenced more leaders and set more attendance records than any other clergyman in American history. National leaders vied for his attention. He was tall, handsome, dashing, sophisticated and intelligent. Hollywood actually tried to cast him in the lead role for the famous movie, "The Robe." He seemed to have had everything.

Graham, Templeton, and Clifford launched out of the starting blocks like Olympic gold medallists in 1945. Why haven't you heard of Chuck Templeton or Bron Clifford? The answer might surprise you.

By 1950 Templeton had left the ministry. He pursued a radio career. He became an announcer and a newscaster, telling the world that he no longer believed Jesus Christ was the Son of God. He became an atheist. By 1950, this future 'Babe Ruth' of preaching was not even in the ball game!

By 1954 Clifford had lost his family, ministry and health. Eventually he lost his life because of addiction to alcohol. Financial irresponsibility left his wife and their two Downs Syndrome children penniless. This once famous preacher, died of cirrhosis of the liver at the age of 35 in a rundown hotel on the edge of Amarillo, Texas. He died a pitiful, dishonorable and unsung death. Some pastors from Amarillo, Texas got together and collected enough money to buy a cheap casket. They shipped his body back to the East Coast, where he was buried in a pauper's cemetery.

In 1945, all three of these men with extraordinary gifts were preaching for the purpose of multiplying the church by thousands of people. But within 10 years, only one of them was still on track for Christ.

"In Christian life it's not how you start, it's how you finish!" A recent survey shocked me; it reported that only one out of ten who start in ministry at the age of 21 serve the Lord to age 65. They fall away from ministry due to immorality, pride, discouragement, liberal theology and a love for wealth and the things of this world."

Favour has brought you this far, focusing on Jesus Christ who has brought you this far is key. Never behave as if you have made it; press on till you close your eyes in death.

> "In Christian life it's not how you start, it's how you finish!"

My advice: keep your focus, keep pressing on for it will not be long.

Prayer: O' Lord help me to finish strong and finish well in Christ and reap the fruits of my labour.

Quotation: *"Start strong, stay strong, and finish strong by remembering why you started in the first place."* -Ralph Marston

33

How Does God Look?

> If you want to know what God looks like, then look to Jesus his look alike.

- ◆ How he lived.
- ◆ How he loved.
- ◆ How he spoke to people.
- ◆ How he forgave.
- ◆ How he showed mercy.
- ◆ How he comforted.
- ◆ How he showed compassion.
- ◆ How he prayed.
- ◆ How he showed kindness.
- ◆ How he taught.
- ◆ How he cared.
- ◆ How he directed people.
- ◆ How he guided people.
- ◆ How he healed.
- ◆ How he committed no sin.
- ◆ How he hated sin but loved sinners.
- ◆ How he took the side of the poor and the weak.
- ◆ How he promised a new creation -a new heaven and earth.
- ◆ How lovingly he introduced the Heavenly Father to people.
- ◆ Jesus is the Word of God in the flesh.

Prayer: Oh Lord help me to look the way you looked; the way Jesus looked.

Quotation: *"And do not be conformed to this world, but be transformed by the renewing of your mind, so that you may prove what the will of God is, that which is good and acceptable and perfect."* -**Paul of Tarsus**

34

This Too Will Pass Away!

"Arise, get thee to Zarephath, which belongeth to Zidon, and dwell there: behold, I have commanded a widow woman there to sustain thee." 1 King 17:9

Elijah was a human being like you and me. As a matter of fact, speaking of Elijah in James 5:17 the Word said he "was a man subject to like passion as we are.." Therefore, if God could sustain him in a time of drought and famine; the same God can sustain you in your dry time. Every human being on the face of the earth will at some point go through a period when they feel downcast and dry. A period when nothing works, no matter how hard they try. A period when they feel all hell has unleashed its wrath upon them and there is no way out. I call it the wilderness experience.

Whenever you get to such a place in your life, it is key that you tell yourself, **'this too will pass away'**. Those were my exact words about 25 years ago. I had started my doctorate in Chemical Engineering at University of Benin earlier in 1989. The first year, they offered me accommodation on the campus, but I did not use it. However, at the last year of the program, I needed to be resident on campus. I remember pleading desperately with an Admin Officer; she was blunt, 'we don't have accommodation for you sir!'

Lo and behold, while leaving the office I saw a banner that reads 'this too will pass away.' I turned to her and said, "Sure. This one will pass away."

Guess what? While sharing my predicament with some of the lecturers in the Chemical Engineering Dept, one of them offered me a two bedroom flat; free of charge. The icing on the cake was, this was a professor with very vast knowledge in the area of my research. We used to study in his house library from night till early in the morning. With the official accommodation, which was located on another Campus I would not have had that privilege.

> "Most challenges have an expiry date including yours"

What I am saying is that whatever is the critical stage of need that seems impossible to meet, it will surely pass away. It is only a passage to a greater place that God has prepared for you. The wilderness experience, the dry times, the period of famine, etc., is only for a period of time; God is taking you to a better place. "Most challenges have an expiry date including yours"

In this, your year and season of prosperity and divine intervention, God is taking you to a place of permanent sustenance, peace, and rest. Whatever the challenge: career based, spiritual, ministerial, matrimonial, financial, physical, health matters, even undefined. It has an expiry date. Hold on and don't give up!

Listen to me, God is changing your status and your situation; your shame will be traded for fame. God is taking you to a place where your influence cannot be measured. He is taking you to a place where your wealth cannot be qualified. You are relocating from lack to supernatural abundance. You are going from prison to palace. God is taking you to a place where sickness, disease, barrenness, joblessness, demonic forces cannot operate in your life.

You are an eagle, you are not a chicken. One of the characteristics of an eagle is that, it is patient and calculating. God will give you the best of things, even those you never prayed for. Just wait, and you will see the glory of thy Lord in the land of the living! It is your season of divine intervention!

Prayer: Oh Lord, in the precious name of Jesus I command these challenges (mention their names) staring me in the face to disappear in the name of Jesus. Let the troubles of my life pass away today in Jesus name.

Quotation: *"You should never view your challenges as a disadvantage. Instead, it's important for you to understand that your experience facing and overcoming adversity is actually one of your biggest advantages."*
-**Michelle Obama**

35

Too Late!

"That night the Lord appeared to Paul and said, 'Be encouraged, Paul. Just as you have been a witness to me here in Jerusalem, you must preach the Good News in Rome as well' 12 The next morning a group of Jews got together and bound themselves with an oath not to eat or drink until they had killed Paul. 13 There were more than forty of them in the conspiracy". Acts 23:11-13

In the ninth chapter of Acts, we read the account of the divine encounter that Saul of Tarsus had, that changed him to Paul of Tarsus. Spiritually, he became born again. Master-wise he changed from being loyal to Satan to being loyal to Jesus. Career-wise he changed from being a 'thug', a hooligan, an area boy in the hand of religious men (I almost said in the hand of politicians)used to arrest and kill their enemies to being a dignified Evangelist, Preacher, Teacher, Bible Author and Missionary of the Lord Jesus Christ.

Have you made that change? When you make that change, heaven details for you angels, not just to protect you, but to herald you, accompany you, surround you, hedge you, guide you and protect you from powers and principalities. The blood of Jesus marks you out as untouchable. The anointing distinguishes. You become a God sent! Heaven monitors you 24/7.

God is constantly planning and sending messages to you and ensuring that you carry out His assignment successfully. That is what happened in the story above. Jesus had just personally appeared to Paul overnight and given him his next assignment, that is, to take the gospel to Rome. Then in the morning, some conspirators gathered and had sworn to an oath that they will neither eat or drink until they kill Paul! What did I hear you say, "too late!"

The Master of the Universe has made his decision, overnight, to make you a visitor to Emperor Caesar!

You are not killable. Too late! You can no more be molested. Too late! Sickness cannot hinder you. Too late! The conspirators, enemies of progress, kidnappers, enchanters, diviners can go on hunger strike for the rest of their lives, they cannot harm or, hurt you. All too late!

The Word says in Isaiah 8:10: *Take counsel together, and it shall come to nought; speak the word, and it shall not stand: for God is with us."*

Too late for you not to fulfill destiny. You have appealed to Caesar and to Caesar you shall go, you are unstoppable!

"Satan you and your cohorts - sorry for you, you are just -too late to stop my progress!"

Verse 13 of Acts 23 gave a very important number. More than 40 people gathered. Each person represents all manner of 'forces' that the enemy wants to throw at you. Yet, it is too late. Jesus took 39 lashes for your sake and he himself stands to defeat the enemy to complete the number.

Relax, co-worker of God, we are on His Highest Imperial Majesty's; the assignment direct from the King of Kings and The Lord of Lord's. We shall succeed! He who called us is able to provide and to guarantee our safety.

Ministerially, matrimonially, academically, professionally, family-wise, I see you succeeding. Look at the One who has sent you, not the one who is wasting his time plotting against you. He that is with you is more than he that is with them.

"Satan you and your cohorts - sorry for you, you are just -too late to stop my progress!"

97

Prayer: Oh Lord let it be too late for my enemies to harm me. O Lord, don't give me over to my stubborn pursuers. No matter the number of people that have sworn to destroy me, O Lord, expose their wickedness and exterminate all of them.

Quotation: *"It doesn't matter if you come from the inner city. People who fail in life are people who find lots of excuses. It's never too late for a person to recognize that they have potential in themselves."* -**Dr. Ben Carson**

36

How Can A Nation
Return To God?

*"Therefore say thou unto them, Thus saith the Lord of hosts;
Turn ye unto me, saith the Lord of hosts, and I will turn unto
you, saith the Lord of hosts." Zechariah 1:2*

We must establish some facts. God does not intend to destroy the
nation and the world anymore. However, God does not want nations to
be against him because nations make the world. If they do He will not
hesitate to destroy them totally or, punish them in one way or the other.
as detailed in Genesis 6 to 9, He destroyed them with the flood.

When the people of Palestine sinned, He displaced them with the Jews.
When the Jews sinned against God, He sent them into exile in Babylon.
So, when God wants a nation to return to Him, what does he do?
We have many examples of different models in the Bible.
God will identify someone He can trust, raise, and send on the assignment.

1. Noah for the entire world.
2. Abraham for Sodom and Gomorrah.
3. Cyrus, Zerrubabel, Ezra, and Nehemiah for the Jews.
4. Jonah for Nineveh.
5. Elijah for Israel.
6. Jeremiah for Israel.
7. Amos for many Nations: Damascus, Gaza, Tyrus, Edom, Ammon,
   Moab, Judah, and Israel.
8. John the Baptist for the Jews.
9. Jesus for the entire world.

He will give the person a message.

1. Repentance: eg. Noah, John the Baptist, Jonah, and Jesus.

2. Warning: eg. Jeremiah and Amos.
3. Intercession: eg. Abraham, Moses, Nehemiah, and Daniel.
4. Futuristic Revelation Warnings: eg. Daniel and John the Baptist.

There are different types of responses that determine the result they have.

1. Refusal to repent leading to total destruction: eg. The Noah generation, the Canaanites, the Jebusites, and the Baal worshippers.
2. Genuine repentance allowing for forgiveness, healing and restoration: eg. The Ninevites.

My message to you my brothers and sisters, pastors and friends:

- God has sent you to this nation to bring it back to him.
- You are the ones who knows what message God has given you for your nation:
- To pray and intercede
- To warn and prophesy
- To plant churches
- To motivate and mobilize others
- To provide resources made from genuine sources to advance the Kingdom.

Let's do it. It is not over for any nation.

There is hope for the nations, From Canada to the USA, UK, Gabon, Tanzania, China, Nigeria and everywhere in between. Wherever God has placed you, you must not give up on the nation. You are the agent of change for the better.

"7 For there is hope of a tree if it be cut down, that it will sprout again, and that the tender branch thereof will not cease. 8 Though the root thereof wax old in the earth, and the stock thereof die in the ground; 9 Yet through the scent of water it will bud, and bring forth boughs like a plant." -Job 14:79

You are not a chicken, you are an eagle, live like one.

Prayer: Oh Lord, let me be an instrument in returning this nation to you. Bring us to eagle positioning.

Quotation: *"If we ever forget that we are One Nation Under God, then we will be a nation gone under."* -**Ronald Reagan**

37

Removing Lunacy Through Praying And Fasting.

"Lord, have mercy on my son: for he is lunatic, and sore vexed: for ofttimes he falleth into the fire, and oft into the water. 16 And I brought him to thy disciples, and they could not cure him.19 Then came the disciples to Jesus apart, and said, Why could not we cast him out?21 Howbeit this kind goeth not out but by prayer and fasting." Matt 17:15-16, 19-21. KJV

Jesus gave us reason for praying and fasting in this 'live' experience where he literarily, removed 'lunacy' from a young boy. This is not a parable. It was a co-op. It was an industrial training session for the disciples- fast tracking it forward for you and I.

> "Praying and fasting has the capacity to suspend the natural and make room for the supernatural."

"Praying and fasting has the capacity to suspend the natural and make room for the supernatural." That was buttress by Jesus when He declared 'this kind' of a healing cannot happen except by prayer and fasting.

There is too much talk about praying, particularly in North America, we are talkers and not doers when it comes to the issue of praying. The least attended Christian event is prayer meetings and least participated Christian spiritual exercise is fasting. No wonder so many comment on what seems to be the powerlessness of our spiritual age.

My advice, let us shift gear from today, from prayerlessness to prayerfulness. From 'fasting-lessness' to 'fasting-fullness.'

As we fast and pray:

♦ The lunacy of our children will disappear.
♦ The lunacy of our spouses will disappear.
♦ The lunacy in the church will disappear.
♦ The lunacy of our parents and relations will disappear.
♦ The lunacy of societies will disappear.
♦ The lunacy in our businesses will disappear. There will be profitability and corresponding prosperity.
♦ The lunacy in government, in the form of corruption, will disappear. Secrets will be revealed and appropriate sanctions will be applied.
♦ The lunacy in our lives will disappear.

When you want lunacy to give way, this day and beyond- Jesus' prescription will help you- take an injection of prayer and fasting. Overdose has a positive effect so not only is it allowed, it is recommended!

I encourage you to join us in Christ Apostolic Church Bethel Toronto, as we annually pray and fast for 21 days March 1-21.

Prayer: Oh Lord, empower me not only to fast and pray regularly but also enable me to get rid of the spirit of lunacy that is so prevalent around and within me.

Quotation: *"Prayer is reaching out after the unseen; fasting is letting go of all that is seen and temporal. Fasting helps express, deepen, confirm the resolution that we are ready to sacrifice anything, even ourselves to attain what we seek for the kingdom of God."* -**Andrew Murray**

38

How To Develop
Godly Character.

"The LORD is the portion of mine inheritance and of my cup: thou maintainest my lot.

6 The lines are fallen unto me in pleasant places; yea, I have a goodly heritage." Psalm 16:5-6

We have a heritage of godly character from our Lord Jesus. As you and I walk in this newness of nature, of godly character in Christ Jesus our heaven shall open. Every power associated with the ungodly character that has tied you down to poverty, wretchedness, and failure, I command them to go in Jesus name. This month you shall soar. This month you shall be lifted high. This month you will be far from oppression in Jesus name. This month your child will graduate from school successfully.

You will not know failure at the point of success. Joseph lived a godly life and his benefactor forgot him temporarily but, at the appointed time he remembered him. He became the agent of change to bring him from prison to palace, opulence, and prosperity. This month as you walk in godly character, your benefactor will remember you for good and you will re-introduce your new self.

- ♦ Take time to pray.
- ♦ Take time to read the Bible, meditate on it, and live it.
- ♦ Take time to fellowship. Go to church and make yourself useful to your maker by serving, giving and helping others.

"Do your work, whether in your office or, private business as unto the Lord, working hard and working smart all in integrity and holiness." Don't be a victim of April fool, but be a fool for Jesus.

This is our month of developing godly character. Remember that the sinless Jesus Christ took the sinful you and me to Golgotha. From that place of the Skull, He blood-washed us to give us a new status of saints!

> "Do your work, whether in your office or, private business as unto the Lord, working hard and working smart all in integrity and holiness."

This month shall be your best month in Jesus name. You are an eagle, you are not a chicken. You will soar.

Prayer: Oh Lord godly character is what I need to live well on earth and to make heaven. Help me Oh Lord to develop godly character.

Quotation: *"When wealth is lost, nothing is lost; when health is lost, something is lost; when character is lost, all is lost."* -**Billy Graham**

39

What Is The One Thing That Can Facilitate Your Making Heaven After All Is Said And Done?

"Jesus answered him, "Truly, truly, I say to you, unless one is born again he cannot see the kingdom of God." John 3:3

"But as for the cowardly, the faithless, the detestable, as for murderers, the sexually immoral, sorcerers, idolaters, and all liars, their portion will be in the lake that burns with fire and sulfur, which is the second death." Rev 21:8

Actually, there are two things we as Christians seek for desperately, particularly we ministers of the gospel; gifts and fruits of the Holy Spirit. And to be honest, we seek more of the gifts than the fruits. The gifts typify our charisma, the fruits our character.

What are the gifts?

"7 But the manifestation of the Spirit is given to every man to profit withal.

8 For to one is given by the Spirit the word of wisdom; to another the word of knowledge by the same Spirit;

9 To another faith by the same Spirit; to another the gifts of healing by the same Spirit;

10 To another the working of miracles; to another prophecy; to another discerning of spirits; to another diverse kind of tongues; to another the interpretation of tongues: 11 But all these worketh that one and the selfsame Spirit, dividing to every man severally as he will." 1 Cor 12:7-12

What are the fruits?

> "If you have to make a decisive choice of making heaven, then from today focus on acquiring the fruits of The Holy Spirit, not the gifts!"

"22 But the fruit of the Spirit is love, joy, peace, longsuffering, gentleness, goodness, faith,

23 Meekness, temperance: against such there is no law." Gal 5:22-23

The truth must be said, you can have all the gifts and go to hell but, you cannot have all the fruits and go to hell!

Jesus said regading those who have the gifts but lack the fruits - Matt 7:21-23 *"I will tell you I never knew you."*

Paul said, regarding the gifts:

"And lest I should be exalted above measure through the abundance of the revelations, there was given to me a thorn in the flesh, the messenger of Satan to buffet me, lest I should be exalted above measure. 8 For this thing, I besought the Lord thrice, that it might depart from me. 9 And he said unto me, My grace is sufficient for thee: for my strength is made perfect in weakness. Most gladly, therefore, will I rather glory in my infirmities, that the power of Christ may rest upon me. 10 Therefore I take pleasure in infirmities, in reproaches, in necessities, in persecutions, in distresses for Christ's sake: for when I am weak, then am I strong." 2 Cor 12:7-10

The long and short of what Paul was saying is, that I focused on the gifts and I got so much of it that God decided to do something to humble me, so that I will not miss eternity. Trust me, there is nothing wrong with having both, but if you really want to have heaven then, work on both. "If you have to make a decisive choice of making heaven, then from today focus on acquiring the fruits of The Holy Spirit, not the gifts!"

This is what we are talking about, when we talk about raising an eagle generation of believers. A new generation of believers that is not charisma driven but, character driven.

So, the one thing that can secure your heavenly ticket: the Fruit of the Holy Spirit.

Prayer: Oh Lord, I need both the gifts and the fruits of the Holy Spirit.

Quotation: *"I would not give one moment of heaven for all the joy and riches of the world, even if it lasted for thousands and thousands of years."* **-Martin Luther**

40

God Can Meet Your Needs

GOD CAN MEET YOUR NEEDS

"Then the foreign rabble who were traveling with the Israelites began to crave the good things of Egypt. And the people of Israel also began to complain. "Oh, for some meat!" they exclaimed." Numbers 11:4 NLT

5 "We remember the fish we used to eat for free in Egypt. And we had all the cucumbers, melons, leeks, onions, and garlic we wanted. 6 But now our appetites are gone." Numbers 11:5-6 KJV

In the early part of this chapter, the people complained of hardship and God punished them with burning fire. Read the scripture above again. You discover that there was a mixed multitude - 'foreign rabble' - that was instigating the Israelites again. Provoking them to make unreasonable demands. Who or, what is provoking you? See Moses' reaction:

"And Moses said to the LORD, "Why are you treating me, your servant, so harshly? Have mercy on me! What did I do to deserve the burden of all these people?12 Did I give birth to them? Did I bring them into the world? Why did you tell

me to carry them in my arms like a mother carries a nursing baby? How can I carry them to the land you swore to give their ancestors? 13 Where am I supposed to get meat for all these people? They keep whining to me, saying, 'Give us meat to eat!' 14 I can't carry all these people by myself! The load is far too heavy! 15 If this is how you intend to treat me, just go ahead and kill me. Do me a favor and spare me this misery!"
Numbers 11:11-15 NLT

Pastor, parent, can you hear yourself in Moses? Pastor, church leader, parent, stop acting God.

Your assignment is to gather information from the people and pass it to God. He can meet your needs as well as theirs! See God's reply:

"And say to the people, 'Purify yourselves, for tomorrow you will have meat to eat. You were whining, and the LORD heard you when you cried, "Oh, for some meat! We were better off in Egypt!" Now the LORD will give you meat, and you will have to eat it. 19 And it won't be for just a day or two, or for five or ten or even twenty. 20 You will eat it for a whole month until you gag and are sick of it. For you have rejected the LORD, who is here among you, and you have whined to him, saying, "Why did we ever leave Egypt?"
Numbers 11:18-20 NLT

How many of us are querying why we are Christians? No matter how desirable the garlic in Egypt was you were a slave there! If you are not in Christ, you are in crisis. Get out of the mentality that you were better off when you were an unbeliever! "The worst of Christians in terms of needs is better than the best of unbeliever with all their worth." God says He can meet your needs, if that is your problem.

> "The worst of Christians in terms of needs is better than the best of unbeliever with all their worth."

Even Moses himself was doubting God's capacity. He was using human logic, full of facts and evidence that showed this is 'impossible' but not for God. Can that be you and I? Moses was not yet finished with God; hear him:

> *"But Moses responded to the LORD, "There are 600,000-foot soldiers here with me, and yet you say, 'I will give them meat for a whole month!' 22 Even if we butchered all our flocks and herds, would that satisfy them? Even if we caught all the fish in the sea, would that be enough?"* Numbers 11:21-22 NLT

Can you imagine human calculations! Can you put yourself in Moses' shoes, how you rationalize?

Can you hear yourself asking the same things? How will I pay my children's school fees? How will I pay my tithe? How will I build a house, get a car, do what's needed?

I love God. The great provider. The El-Shaddai! Here is the reply to Moses' mathematical calculations of God's inability, and seeming incapability to meet human needs in general, and your needs in particular: *"Then the LORD said to Moses, "has my arm lost its power? Now you will see whether or not my word comes true!"* Numbers 11:23. Friends, I submit to you and myself that, His arms have not lost power over our needs. Even though your needs and my needs are unreasonable! See God at work:

> *"So the people went out and caught quail all that day and throughout the night and all the next day, too. No one gathered less than fifty bushels! They spread the quail all around the camp to dry."* Numbers 11:32 [NLT]

"God can and shall surely meet your needs! In fact He will surely exceed your expectations."

I prophesy to you today, you will go out and find 'quails' within your reach. You will gather more than you will need.

That job will come! That pregnancy will come! You will pass that exam! That debt will be paid! That divorce paper will be torn! That prodigal son will come back! You will have a good husband/wife! That business and ministry will blossom! The garlic and onions that once attracted you to sin will be provided for you in Christ. "God can and shall surely meet your needs! In fact He will surely exceed your expectations."

Prayer: Oh Lord you exceeded the expectations of the Israelites and gave them quails. Oh Lord I pray, today give me quails but not in your anger.

Quotation: *"We can be certain that God will give us the strength and resources we need to live through any situation in life that he ordains. The will of God will never take us where the grace of God cannot sustain us."* **-Billy Graham**

41

Meeting Jesus in Galilee

"And go quickly, and tell his disciples that he is risen from the dead; and, behold, he goeth before you into Galilee; there shall ye see him: lo, I have told you. 10 Then said Jesus unto them, Be not afraid: go tell my brethren that they go into Galilee, and there shall they see me." Matthew 28:7,10 KJV

Growing up in the church back in Nigeria, Easter Monday is usually spent meeting Jesus in Galilee. Usually, on a designated prayer mountain where we pray for the individual, the church, and the nation! Today, such traditional worship style is fading away. May I suggest, that we still in our individual and family altars find time to meet Jesus today in our Galilee!

Particularly, let us pray for Canada or whatever your nation may be!

♦ That God will give the Prime Minister and his cabinet wisdom to rule well
♦ Pray that the Members of Parliament and Members of Provincial Parliament and Councillors will legislate well
♦ Let us pray that the Premiers and Mayors will rule with the fear of God
♦ Pray against budget deficits, federally, provincially and in all municipalities
♦ In 1911 98% of Christians in Canada went to church. Now, it is less than 6%, let us pray for revival and resurrection
♦ Pray that Canada will return to their Maker. Canada will find God afresh again and our values will glorify God
♦ Pray for yourself, that God will revive you in Jesus name
♦ Pray for the peace of Jerusalem

Happy meeting with Jesus in Galilee. It is not out of place if you meet God in Galilee. I recommend for the church to start that practice again where Easter Monday is not just spent eating and drinking in the

> "Let us meet Jesus in Galilee."

eateries around town but that people meet in Recreational Centers and Parks and eat spiritual food. "Let us meet Jesus in Galilee."

Prayer: Oh Lord I don't want to meet you in Galilee once a year but every day.

Quotation: *"As on the Sea of Galilee, the Christ is whispering "Peace."* -**John Greenleaf Whittier**

42

How Are You Spending Your Days?

"They would spend the night around the house of God, since it was their duty to guard it and to open the gates every morning." 1 Chronicles 9:27 NLT

The books of Chronicles, Ezra and Nehemiah were all concerned with the return of people of the Israel who had gone into exile. While Zerubbabel was concerned about building the physical temple, and Nehemiah the physical gates, Ezra was concerned about spirituality of the people he was concerned about their return mentally to keep God's word. There were other people who were engaged through the division of labour. The above scripture talks about the Levites, among the Levites. those who were gatekeepers could be found.

Growing up in church in my day was different from what it is today. Churches were not in plazas and malls. Churches were in designated freehold buildings. Not only that, they also usually built separate buildings like mission houses behind the main auditorium as well as an additional tall narrow building that housed a big bell. This bell was kept by church gate keepers who would ring it at the time of evening service and most especially in the morning to wake up church members. They would be rung twice: 4:30am and 5.00am, when the service starts. Growing up, my father was the gate keeper for our community church. When he returned from ringing the bell by 4:30am he would wake us up to do our family devotion and by 5am we would follow him to church.

"They would spend the night around the house of God, since it was their duty to guard it and to open the gates every morning." How are you spending your days? Your evenings? Your mornings? Are you one of God's gate keepers?

My father told me a story that I want to share about being faithful as a gate keeper. He said that though he himself did not go to school, he vowed that each of his children would. He was a carpenter and farmer. I was the first son. The little money he was making with his combined occupations could not pay my school fees. So, he decided to go for a third one. There was a school called Ekiti Baptist Boys High School in our town of Igede-Ekiti. He told me that he had decided to apply to be a gateman there. He went for the interview and got the job! He was very happy, but that night he slept and had a very special visitor. He said he had a dream and a man in glowing white garment appeared to him. Asked him why he went to seek for the job of a gate keeper in the school? He explained that it was in an effort to save enough money to send his son to school. The man asked him who will be the gate keeper for the church, who would ring the bell in the evening and the mornings? He said he warned him not to take the job, that he would provide money for him to send his children to school. He should continue to be the church gate keeper.

God was faithful to my father and he was able to send me to secondary school, tertiary institutions and to the glory of God I have a Ph.D. as well as a post doctoral degree in Chemical Engineering. Maybe I would not be writing to you this morning if I did not go to school. If my father refused to heed the warning and abandoned the work God gave him. Thank God he was a faithful gate keeper.

In our time, there are still the Ezras, Zerubbabels and Nehemiahs. They are the popular General Overseers, Archbishops, and Apostles who you hear about today. But there were other Levites and priests whose names were not mentioned. Others who spent their evenings around God's house and kept the gates in the morning. They are all part of the building project and process. God is watching you. Are you a volunteer in church? Are you engaged in para-ministry, or even in the "marketplace ministry," which is a secular job? God wants you to be around his house in the evening, praying and interceding. God wants you to open the gate of his church for many that are yet to know him in the morning. God wants you to ring the bell around the world that Jesus saves.

How are you spending your days? "Are you leaving your God ordained purpose in the pursuit of money?" Do you realize that Nehemiah was the cup bearer to the king? In today's nomenclature he would be referred to as the Minister of Home Affairs, Special Adviser to the President, or the Secretary of Treasury? Which would have been a major position. But that was not his purpose, his purpose was to be around the house of God and rebuild the gate. I repeat, my question this morning is: how are you spending your days?

Like the days of old, the gates of the nations, churches, families, are destroyed, the buildings are falling down. God has stirred up the heart of Cyrus to mobilize men to action. May you be one of those ones who will spend their nights around God's house and in the mornings open the gate!

> "Are you leaving your God ordained purpose in the pursuit of money?"

Every third weekend in September we gather in Toronto on the platform of the International Gathering of Eagles Conference to strategize on how to repair the falling altars. Please join us for what promises to be an amazing time of great power and refreshing a time when God will raise up Eagle Believers and empower dedicated men and women for the building of his church. This is an annual interdenominational Conference for pastors, church workers and all members of the body of Christ that want to see revival in our day. Iron sharpens iron. Be there. Be blessed. For more info visit www.igoeministry.com.

Prayer: Oh Lord. Make me a gate keeper not only for the church but also for the nations. Make me a partaker of the International Gathering of Eagle Conferences. Help me to join Pastor Amos Dada and his team in raising an Eagle Generation and travel around the nations to propagate your gospel.

Quotation: Go ye therefore, and teach all nations, baptizing them in the name of the Father, and of the Son, and of the Holy Ghost -Jesus Christ

43

Destroy Sin Before It Destroys You

"The sting of death is sin; and the strength of sin is the law."
1 Cor 15:56 KJV

"For the wages of sin is death; but the gift of God is eternal life through Jesus Christ our Lord." Rom. 6:23 KJV

- Sin destroys
- Sin defiles
- Sin brings bondage
- Sin demotes
- Sin blocks breakthroughs
- Sin will rob you of joy and peace
- Sin has a dangerous appeal and dangerous consequences
- Sin destroyed the anointing on Samson
- Sin dented the great career, image and name of David
- Sin turned the heart of Solomon from God
- Sin committed by Jeroboam led Israel to sin
- Sin destroyed King Ahab's dynasty
- Sin destroyed the Kingdom of King Saul
- Sin of Eli's sons terminated his ministry, brought sudden death, ended his family's calling caused the glory of God to depart
- Sin led to the destruction of the first world by flood
- Sin led to the destruction of Sodom and Gomorrah
- Sin destroyed the future of Reuben and his generation
- Sin has destroyed many marriages and led to countless divorces
- Sin of parents have destroyed the future of many promising children
- Sin destroys homes, families, and relationships
- Sin has led to sudden death of many young and old

- Sin has destroyed the Ministry of many high profile ministers throughout time
- Sin is a block to your passport to Heaven
- Sin is actually the passport and visa to hell
- Sin has destroyed the destiny of countless individuals
- Sin has nothing to offer more than momentary pleasure followed by a life of regrets and condemnation to hell fire
- "SIN= Success In Nothing
- SIN= Satan's Identification Number"

Only the fools engage in sin. The wise avoid it like a plague. The way you treat sin shows whether you are a fool or a wise person. The wise see sin and flee, the foolish ones take the bait and are captured by Satan.

God loves sinners but hates sin. Sin has an antidote and certified remedy in Christ:

"SIN= Success In Nothing

"For God so loved the world that he gave his one and only Son, that whoever believes in him shall not perish but have eternal life." John 3:16 NASB

"For sin shall not have dominion over you: for ye are not under the law but under grace..." Rom 6:14 KJV

SIN= Satan's Identification Number"

"Jesus is the only way out of sin" John 14:6 KJV

Destroy sin before it destroys you. You have been warned!

Prayer: O Lord I have had so much of the destructive power of sin, give me grace to overcome sin.

Quotation: "*...how then can I do this great wickedness, and sin against God? I would rather die than do something which I know to be a sin, or, to be against God's will.*" **-Joan of Arc**

44

Too Anointed

"But the anointing which ye have received of him abideth in you, and ye need not that any man teach you: but as the same anointing teacheth you of all things, and is truth, and is no lie, and even as it hath taught you, ye shall abide in him." 1 John 2:27

I am just TOO anointed:

- Too to be tormented. Too anointed to be caged.
- Too anointed to be put to shame. Too anointed to be frustrated.
- Too anointed to be stagnated. Too anointed to be embarrassed.
- Too anointed to be misdirected. Too anointed to be manipulated.
- Too anointed to be cursed. Too anointed to be wasted.
- Too anointed to waste away. Too anointed to be tied down.
- Too anointed to fail. Too anointed to be defeated.
- Too anointed to be fooled. Too anointed to be pushed around by witches and wizards.
- Too anointed to be in bondage and captivity. Too anointed to be sick and stressed
- Too anointed to mess up my destiny with destiny killers and wasters.
- Too anointed to waste my time looking for babalawos (herbalists), secret cults, freemansons and voodooist for help in life.
- Too anointed to waste my anointing and destiny on the lap of Delilah.
- "Too anointed to live my life committing sin and wallowing in corruption."
- Too anointed not to pray, read the bible, meditate on it and live it.
- Too anointed not to be faithful in giving to God and the gospel, especially through tithing.
- Too anointed not to prosper in this world and sponsor God's projects.
- Too anointed not to preach the gospel and bring souls to God.

> "Too anointed to live my life committing sin and wallowing in corruption."

♦ Too anointed not to know that this world will soon pass away and that Jesus is coming back.

♦ Too anointed not to know that God has a purpose for me and this world and I must fulfill purpose.

♦ Too anointed not to know that extramarital affairs have the potential to derail my marriage and lead me to divorce.

♦ Too anointed not to know that I am responsible to bring up my children in a godly fashion.

♦ Too anointed to miss heaven and go to hell.

♦ Too anointed... (add your own to the list)

Why are we too anointed?

1. God is for us: Rom 8:31
2. God is with us: John 14:23
3. God is in us:1 John 4:4

> *"But ye are a chosen generation, a royal priesthood, an holy nation, a peculiar people; that ye should shew forth the praises of him who hath called you out of darkness into his marvellous light;" 1 Pet 2:9* KJV

Take time to reflect on this refrain from "I Know Who I am" by Sinach:

> *"I know who God says I am*
> *What He says I am*
> *Where He says I'm at*
> *I know who I am"*

Prayer: Oh Lord help me to know who I am, that I am anointed. Help me to have fresh anointing.

Quotation: *"When the anointing of God is upon a person, it changes that individual from being a little ordinary person into being a giant."* *-Unknown Pastor*

45

What Are You Anointed For?

"The Spirit of the Lord God is upon me; because the Lord hath anointed me to preach good tidings unto the meek; he hath sent me to bind up the brokenhearted, to proclaim liberty to the captives, and the opening of the prison to them that are bound;2 To proclaim the acceptable year of the Lord, and the day of vengeance of our God; to comfort all that mourn;3 To appoint unto them that mourn in Zion, to give unto them beauty for ashes, the oil of joy for mourning, the garment of praise for the spirit of heaviness; that they might be called trees of righteousness, the planting of the Lord, that he might be glorified. And they shall build the old wastes, they shall raise up the former desolations, and they shall repair the waste cities, the desolations of many generations" -Isaiah 61:1-4

- I am anointed to lift up the name of Jesus.
- I am anointed for the ministry of reconciliation (i.e. reconciling men to God).
- I am anointed to break barriers in my generation.
- I am anointed to raise champions.
- I am anointed to preach the gospel to the meek.
- I am anointed to set the captives free.
- I am anointed to open the prison gates to them that are bound.
- I am anointed to bring healing to the hurting.
- I am anointed to be a blessing to my generation.
- I am anointed for the benefit of nations and kingdoms.
- I am anointed to uproot negative powers and principalities.
- I am anointed to pull down strongholds.
- I am anointed to destroy yokes.
- I am anointed to throw down satanic altars, wherever they may be found.
- I am anointed to plant the good seed of the gospel.

♦ I am anointed to build a generation of people and leaders of integrity.
♦ I am anointed to build a people that will build the nations.
♦ I am anointed to lift up the name of Jesus.
♦ I am anointed to proclaim liberty to the captives.
♦ I am anointed to preach the gospel to my generation.
♦ I am anointed to be a voice for my generation.

> "I am anointed to raise a Generation of Eagle Believers"

♦ I am anointed to preach the gospel around the world.
♦ I am anointed to be an ambassador for Jesus.
♦ I am anointed to raise disciples of Jesus Christ in this generation.
♦ I am anointed to intercede for this generation.
♦ "I am anointed to raise a Generation of Eagle Believers"
♦ I am anointed to be a witness that there is no other name whereby we can be saved than the name of Jesus.
♦ I am anointed to… (add your own to the list!)

You must know your purpose, what you are wired and anointed to do in your generation!

Prayer: Oh Lord let me fulfill the purpose of my anointing.

Quotation: *"We are anointed for our assignment on earth because the anointed King lives in us—He is fulfilling His will through us."* **-E.N. Supen**

46

What Is Your Motive?

"Ask all the people of the land and the priests, 'When you fasted and mourned in the fifth and seventh months for the past seventy years, was it really for me that you fasted'. -Zech 7:5 NIV

In your personal walk with God, the motive and intention of your heart is of utmost importance. God does not look at the outward appearance, but He looks at the heart to weigh the motive that drives all external appearances. This is why it is crucial that from your heart, you should direct your outward appearance unto the Lord.

It must never be your intention to impress anyone. You must never aim at pleasing anybody or, creating impressions. No. Rather fellowship with God and be truly sincere in your heart, in seeking His help. He said in His word, that you will find Him when you seek Him with all your heart.

Henceforth:

♦ Before you do that church program, ask yourself what is the motive?

♦ Before you give that gift, ask yourself what is the motive?

- Before you fast and pray that prayer, ask yourself what is the motive?
- Before you embark on that journey, ask yourself what is the motive?
- Before you say what you want to say, ask yourself what is the motive?
- Before you aspire for that desire, ask yourself what is the motive?
- Before you aspire for that political office, ask yourself what is the motive?
- Before you apply for that loan, what is your motive?
- Before you apply for that job, what is your motive?
- Before you preach that sermon, what is your motive?
- Before you lead that protest, what is your motive?
- Before you give that tithe, what is your motive?
- Before you buy and wear that seductive designer dress, what is your motive?
- Before you marry that person, what is your motive?
- Before you carry out that strong impression on your heart, ask yourself what is the motive?

There is a trend nowadays that I find highly disturbing regarding what some people post on their Facebook and other social media profiles. There are some who are posting nude pictures or photos of them engaging in all sorts of immoral and profane acts, whether it be of a sexual nature or involving drugs, alcohol, etc. Others are even taking this one step further and posting such photos of ex-partners, ex-spouses, ex-friends or anyone who has offended them. Why? For cheap popularity? A few more Instagram likes? Short term satisfaction in revenge? Before you post the next thing on your social media, ask yourself what is the motive? In all that you are doing, let your desire be to honour, please and glorify the Lord in everything and he will come through for you.

> *"Thou art worthy, O Lord, to receive glory and honour and power: for thou hast created all things, and for thy pleasure, they are, and were created."* -Rev 4:11 KJV

Let us raise an eagle generation. A saintly, holy, integrity oriented, corruption-free, profane-free generation. Not a chicken generation. Many of you shut your heavens by your ill motives! This is your season of open heavens, watch your motive.

Prayer: Oh Lord give me a pure heart. Keep me pure.

Quotation: *"The moment there is suspicion about a person's motives, everything he does becomes tainted."* **-Mahatma Gandhi**

47

Do Not Backslide

"Thine own wickedness shall correct thee, and thy backslidings shall reprove thee: know therefore and see that it is an evil thing and bitter, that thou hast forsaken the Lord thy God, and that my fear is not in thee, saith the Lord God of hosts."
Jer 2:19

- Backsliding is turning away from God.
  - › *"And the Lord was angry with Solomon, because his heart was turned from the Lord..."* 1 King 11: 9 KJV
- Backsliding is growing cold and leaving the first love.
  - › *"Nevertheless I have somewhat against thee, because you have left thy first love."* Rev 2:4 BRG
- Backsliding is rebelling against the word of God.
  - › *"...Must you rebel forever? Your head is injured, and your heart is sick"* Isaiah 1:5 NLT
- Backsliding is turning from the simplicity of the Gospel, to salvation by law and works.
  - › *"… whosoever of you are justified by the law; you are fallen from grace."* Gal 5: 4.

- Backsliding is one sin that separates a believer from the Lord.
  - › *"But your iniquities have separated between you and your God." Isaiah 59:2*
- Backsliding is turning away from anything good. Turning from your values, and god values.
  - › *"For it is impossible to bring back to repentance those who were once enlightened—those who have experienced the good things of heaven and shared in the Holy Spirit, who have tasted the goodness of the word of God and the power of the age to come—and who then turn away from God...."* Heb 6:4-6 NLT
- Generally, backsliding is growing cold and losing interest in the Lord, the Bible, prayer, church attendance, witnessing and going back to the world. to do the wrong things you had abandoned for Jesus Christ.
  - › *"Because thou sayest, I am rich, and increased with goods, and have need of nothing; and knowest not that thou art wretched, and miserable, and poor, and blind, and naked:"* Rev 3:17 KJV
- Have you backslidden? Stop it now. Return to your Maker today! Rather than be part of the generation of backsliders, be part of a generation of them that seek Him. Psalm 24:6
  - › *"I counsel thee to buy of me gold tried in the fire, that thou mayest be rich; and white raiment, that thou mayest be clothed, and that the shame of thy nakedness do not appear; and anoint thine eyes with eyesalve, that thou mayest see."* Rev 3:18

Friend, you cannot afford to backslide, for all backsliders will go to hell. You will not go to hell in Jesus name!

Prayer: I reject the spirit of backsliding.

Quotations: *"Remember that if you are a child of God, you will never be happy in sin. You are spoiled for the world, the flesh, and the devil. When you were regenerated there was put into you a vital principle, which can* *never be content to dwell in the dead world. You will have to come back, if indeed you belong to the family."* -**Charles Spurgeon**

"When you are not sure of your salvation, it is very easy to get discouraged and to backslide." - **Zac Poonen**

48

What Is Prayer?

"And this is the confidence that we have in him, that, if we ask any thing according to his will, he heareth us." 1 John 5:14

I thought prayer was a necessity for result-oriented people.

But, prayer is about encountering God and growing in relationship with him. It is the means through which we feel His presence, and receive His love as we gain an understanding of what He is like. It is the time when we receive fresh insight into His heart, and new ideas and desires in our hearts are formed; so that we may commune deeply with him.

Prayer is an invocation or act that seeks to activate a rapport with an object of worship through deliberate communication. Prayer can be a form of religious practice, may be either individual or communal and take place in public or in private. It means speaking the words within your heart to God after having grasped His will. Communing with God according to the method laid out in His word. Prayer is not complicated. It can be formal or informal. It is simply a request for help or expression of thanks addressed to God. One of the mistakes we often make concerning prayer is viewing God as an object, a distant personality. an inanimate object, or an unappreciable force. In reality, God is a father, and one even more glorious than the best we could find on earth. Without this understanding, prayer is reduced to a ding-dong affair. So prayer is talking to our father and our father talking to us. It is a two way process/traffic. Any of the two parties can initiate communication. Once you familiarize yourself with this idea, you can expect God to talk to you. To send you errands, show you things and get his wishes done. Just as you get God to meet your needs.

|This leads me to another thought on prayer that I would like to share, which I like to call the telephone concept. You can use your phone anywhere and you can express your wish on your phone to the person on the other line. Today, we use wireless phones and I know that I, for one, am quite glad to have lived in a time with Alexander Bell's great invention. But before Bell, God has been talking to us wirelessly and vice versa. Long ago, Moses wrote the Pentateuch, The Torah, the first five books of the Bible., but how was he able to get such detailed information from God? Because prayer is holding God's attention and getting feedback from him! How is it that Moses was able to get such volumes upon volumes of discussion with God and we struggle with just tidbits of conversation? We need to take advantage of the great privilege we have in being able to pray anytime, anyhow and anywhere- whether it be in the car, the toilet, the open field, the church, etc., God will hear. Praying is like talking to your best friend, parent, or relative all the time as though they were right beside you. If you believe that God lives within your soul, communicating with God all the time becomes easy. Prayer is more than asking God for things, more than texting Him with a "need this" or "thanks for that." It is communion with our God in the splendor of His glory and the expression of His care. Our goals in prayer are to grow in the knowledge of our God, to reflect on the revelation in His Word, in His creation, in His providence, and in His Son. Prayer positions us to be energized, and to truly love God and people.

> *"Ask, and it shall be given you; seek, and ye shall find; knock, and it shall be opened unto you:8 For every one that asketh receiveth; and he that seeketh findeth; and to him that knocketh it shall be opened.9 Or what man is there of you, whom if his son ask bread, will he give him a stone?10 Or if*

he ask a fish, will he give him a serpent? 11 If ye then, being evil, know how to give good gifts unto your children, how much more shall your Father which is in heaven give good things to them that ask him"
-Matthew 7:7-11

There are different levels to prayer, namely: asking, seeking and knocking, which grow in that order. There are also a variety of types of prayer we can engage in, including: prophetic, dangerous, binding & loosing, and authoritative prayers as well as prayers of sanctification, adoration, thanksgiving, and consecration. Additionally, prayer-less Christians are just cheap material for the devil and his cohort. So we all just need to pray! If you're finding it difficult to pray, join a prayer line, attend prayer meetings and/or get a prayer partner.

Prayer: O' Lord, just as you taught the disciples how to pray. Lord teach me how to pray. How to pray for my life, my family, my church and my nation. More than anything O' Lord hear my prayer when I pray.

Quotations: *"The prayer offered to God in the morning during your quiet time is the key that unlocks the door of the day. Any athlete knows that it is the start that ensures a good finish."* - **Adrian Rogers**

"Prayer is not asking. Prayer is putting oneself in the hands of God, at His disposition, and listening to His voice in the depth of our hearts." -**Mother Teresa**

49

How to Be Poor

"Then I said, "They are only the poor, They are foolish; For they do not know the way of the LORD Or the ordinance of their God" -Jer 5:4

"How long wilt thou sleep, O sluggard? when wilt thou arise out of thy sleep?10 Yet a little sleep, a little slumber, a little folding of the hands to sleep: 11 So shall thy poverty come as one that travelleth, and thy want as an armed man." -Prov 6:9-11

Acronym of **POOR**:

P- assing
O- ver
O- pportunities
R- epeatedly

Acronym of **LAZY**:

L- ay aside what you can do and refuse to do it.
A- im at nothing and expect the world to fall into your lap.
Z- eal for nothing.
Y- ou are the architect of your poverty.

Prayer: O' Lord, deliver me from laziness and consequently poverty.

Quotations: *"If you are born poor its not your mistake., but if you die poor it is your mistake."* **-Bill Gates**

50

How Do I Become An Eagle Believer

"But they that wait upon the Lord shall renew their strength; they shall mount up with wings as eagles; they shall run, and not be weary; and they shall walk, and not faint." Isaiah 40:31

I hear people say it is very difficult to be a good Christian, but I don't think so. As a matter of fact it is very difficult *not* to be a good Christian.) It is just like saying education is expensive, and such people are advised to try ignorance. The most important step is accepting Jesus, which you have already done.

The most critical part of a human being is to be born. Once they are on planet earth, call it a struggle but s/he continues to live.

Bill Gates was credited as saying "if you are born poor it is not your mistake, but if you die poor it's your mistake."

In other words, you can be born a chicken with low capacity to fly but, you do not need to die as a chicken, you can transform to an eagle. If you want to become a champion and win Olympic gold medals, with an attitude that, though difficult it is achievable, you will get there. On the other hand, if you think it is difficult but not achievable, you will never get there. The secret of all champions is dedication and consistency, which is really a matter of making key habits.

Bear in mind, being a good Christian is simply not living in sin and doing whatever God tells you to do. Develop these godly habits and guess what? You will become an eagle believer.

1. **Read.** Study and meditate on the Bible daily, and do what the Holy Spirit tells you to do. Acts 11:17; Joshua 1:8
2. **Pray.** Pray for yourself, your family, your church, your community, your nation and your continent. Pray scripturally. Pray not only for yourself but for others. 1 Thes 5:17, Lk 18:1.

3. **Fellowship.** Go to a bible believing church and be involved. Heb 10. 25

4. **Witness.** To witness is to testify about what you know or have experienced. Jesus says, once you have experienced the new birth, go ahead and share the experience. Not only does He does command it, He also gave you the power and ability to do it.
   "But you will receive power when the Holy Spirit comes upon you. And you will be my witnesses, telling people about me everywhere— in Jerusalem, throughout Judea, in Samaria, and to the ends of the earth." Acts 1:8

5. **Witness Christ.** Share whatever you learn. Learn to tell someone about Jesus. Don't be ashamed. Acts 8, Mark 16: 15; Matt 28:19, Rom 1:16

6. **Give.** No man is an island unto himself. Whether you like it or not, we are all wired to give, it is a function of what and whom you give to and the quantity and quality of what you give. The difference is that, in Christian giving you are encouraged to give to a good cause, that is, towards the gospel. Don't be stingy with God. For instance, give (not pay) your tithe to the Lord. If you don't give it to Him, you will give it to the devil who is nothing but a devourer. Lk 6:38

When you do this habitually and not just occasionally, your life will be totally transformed. You will no more be a chicken picking pebbles and dirt, you will become an eagle believer, soaring for the Lord in every area of your life. For if the Holy Ghost burns through you, it will consume the chaff in the life of many.

Prayer: O' Lord make me an eagle Christian. I am tired of being a chicken. I want to become an eagle. Make me an eagle.

Quotations: *"And every one had four faces: the first face was the face of a cherub, and the second face was the face of a man, and the third the face of a lion, and the fourth the face of an eagle."* – **Ezekiel 10:14**

"Eagles: when they walk, they stumble. They are not what one would call graceful. They were not designed to walk. They fly. And when they fly, oh, how they fly, so free, so graceful. They see from the sky what we never see." – **Unknown**

51

Acronym Of An Eagle

"You yourselves have seen what I did to Egypt, and how I carried you on eagles' wings and brought you to myself."
Exodus 19:4

How do we become eagle believers and raise an eagle generation?

E- xcellence. Develop the spirit of excellence. The eagle is a symbol of excellence, not the mundane or mediocre. Reprogram your mind. The mind is the control tower of life. Decisions determine actions, which in turn affect other actions long after. The person each of us will be 20 years from now, is impacted by how we think today. If we want our future to be pleasing to the Lord, then we must begin at once to program our mind with godly thoughts. Read Romans 12:2 and Ephesians 4:23. Open your minds to biblical attitudes, teachings, and philosophies. Life is about pleasing God, not your government, parents or friends.

If a lifestyle is against God, you must be against it. There is a satanic move in our generation that is popular, broad, convenient, easy, illogical and dangerous. It will take godly thoughts to reject this movement. We must reject evil thoughts as laid out in 2 Corinthians 10:5

A- ddition. Learn to add to your level of virtue and faith. 2 Peter 1:5says, *"and beside this, giving all diligence, add to your faith virtue; and to virtue knowledge."* And 2 Peter 1:4 says*"whereby are given unto us exceeding great and precious promises: that by these ye might be partakers of the divine nature, having escaped the corruption that is in the world through lust."*

The eagle does not stay in one place expecting miracles. It sights a prey afar off and goes for it. They don't miss their target. Maybe it's a fresh business, that you need to allow your faith to reach. Fresh church you need to plant. Fresh mandate in your school. Fresh injection of love to your marriage, to make it work. Fresh determination to succeed. The secret is, adding knowledge. How? Follow the Scripture, the instruction manual for our control tower:

1. Seek God's knowledge and apply it. Read Proverbs 2:1-5 and Luke 2:40. If Jesus. John and Samuel all increased in knowledge, why do we think we do not need to?
2. Seek afresh the power of the Holy Ghost.
3. We must approach unbelievers as mere humans, not as potential converts. The strategies of missionaries: They leave their environment, go to others, learn their language.

G- lorify God. Learn to worship God. Psalm 96:1-9 "If you take God for granted, you will be grounded." I say this often. You have a baby for dedication, a marriage, a thanksgiving, an anniversary, or a birthday and come to celebrate it in the church. You call a party outside, spending thousands of dollar to cook for the entire community. Then, you put just $20 or $50 in the thanksgiving offering tray. You are mocking God, not glorifying God. Giving to God is glorifying God, with our substance and talent. Then glorify God in your body by keeping it holy. God cursed Cain because he did not glorify him with his substance.

> "If you take God for granted, you will be grounded."

L- ove God -John 3:16

1 Corinthians 13:4-5 says, *"charity suffereth long, and is kind; charity envieth not; charity vaunteth not itself, is not puffed up. Doth not behave itself unseemly, seeketh not her own, is not easily provoked, thinketh no evil;"*

Love should motivate us to reach our eternity in hell. Love the dying. Love God enough to offer sacrifices for him. Love God enough to give to the gospel. Love God enough to go to the streets, byways, schools, Islamic strongholds, heathenic strongholds, Sikhs, shintos, Asia, Africa, and Australia to proclaim Jesus.

E- xemplify your faith. Live your faith. Showcase your faith. The eagle is the king of birds in the air. He lives like a king. Soars with majesty. You are the king of the earth. You have intellectual prowess. You can make things happen. Challenge yourself to go higher in faith. Challenge yourself to win souls for the master. The eagle refuses to grow old. Henews himself. Withdraws to a secluded place and removes the old talons, feathers, beak and begins to reach new heights. You can reach a new height.

Prayer: Oh Lord make me an eagle.

Quotations:*"The future is as blank as a plain sheet if you don't have an eagle's eye, that's why you should climb to a vantage point to get a good perspective view at your future."* — **Michael Bassey Johnson**

"Like the grand eagle, you spread your wings, and put forth the effort to do great things." -**Richelle E. Goodrich, Making Wishes**

52

What Prosperous People Do Habitually & Faithfully

"But solid food is for the mature, who because of practice have their senses trained to discern good and evil."
Heb 5:14 [NASB]

Six things that characterize godly and prosperous people:

1. They are givers.
2. They are tithers.
3. They are prayer warriors.
4. They are students of the Bible.
5. They are true worshippers.
6. They are diligent in what they do (including career and business)

Do you want to prosper? Engage yourself on these levels, it is a function of time; you will swim in clean money.

Show me a prosperous person, I will show you Christian people who practice these six faithfully and habitually.

Prayer: Give me grace O' Lord, to practice all these. Help me to take up more positive habits and cause me to prosper.

Quotation: *"In truth, the only difference between those who have failed and those who have succeeded lies in the difference of their habits. Good habits are the key to all success. Bad habits are the unlocked door to failure. Thus, the first law I will obey, which precedeth all others is – I will form good habits and become their slave."* **-Og Mandino**

53

The Power Of Service

"Behold, I stand here by the well of water; and the daughters of the men of the city come out to draw water:

14 And let it come to pass, that the damsel to whom I shall say, Let down thy pitcher, I pray thee, that I may drink; and she shall say, Drink, and I will give thy camels drink also: let the same be she that thou hast appointed for thy servant Isaac; and thereby shall I know that thou hast shewed kindness unto my master." Gen 24:13-14.

Read the passage again. What did the Holy Spirit minister to you? Do you remember who is saying that prayer? Do you know his purpose? That was Abraham's chief servant and most senior protocol officer. His master said, 'go and get a wife for my son Isaac from my kindred.'

The Holy Spirit taught me many things here. Let me break them down.

Our criteria for choosing spouses today is far from biblical Firstly, when you tell some Christian folks to marry Christians they question the rational. Must she/he be born again? The answer is 'yes.' Abraham said go to my (Christian) family. Secondly, our focus is on external beauty. What are the body statistics? What is the racial background? Black, white or brown? Thirdly, how smart? What academic achievemnts? How is their intelligence? Fourthly, how fat is the pocket? What is the salary or wages? 3, 4, 5, 6 or 7 figures? How financial stability? Olorunsogo or Surulere (ready-made or starting together)?

Let us look at how Isaac chose: The summary of his prayer, "O Lord show me a lady who can serve!" It is very easy to give a cup of water to a human being who is thirsty, to drink. After one or two cups he will be satisfied but, imagine giving a Camel water!

It reminds me of an incident, when I was doing my Masters in the early 1980s, when one of our mentors got a research contract with a Nigerian brewery in Apapa Lagos. We traveled from Ile-Ife to the Apapa factory. On arrival, we were taken to their bar and were told we were free to drink, free of charge. "You can't be serious," we replied. "we will show you because we are four thirsty young men here today." We boasted! As Christians though, beer and other alcoholic drinks were off limits so we settled for Malt. I downed the first bottle of this chilling drink with speed. Then I noticed, my speed was drastically reduced for the second bottle. You will not believe it, I could not manage to finish three bottles of Malt at one sitting!

Since that day I learnt a lesson, I said to myself, "this world is worth nothing." So, how do you enjoy this world, when you cannot even drink free non alcoholic drinks? There is a limit to what you can drink or eat! No matter how abundant they are, willing you are to consume, there is a maximum!

Abraham's servant chose Rebecca for Isaac because she was willing not just to serve man, but even his animals!

- ◆ Wonder why your marriage is not working, as a man or woman? You are not willing to serve your spouse.
- ◆ Wonder why you were retrenched in that office? You are not serving or at least not to the capacity expected of you.
- ◆ Wonder why you lost that political post? You never served the people, you were serving your belly at the expense of the masses.
- ◆ Wonder why you are not growing in faith? You are not willing to serve in the church.
- ◆ Wonder why you are running from church to church? You have not found where to serve or, you
- ◆ are unwilling to serve. You have been in church for the past 10, 5, 2 years and you have refused to join any department to serve; how can you grow? It is important to know worship is service, giving offering and tithes is service!
- ◆ Wonder why things are not working for you generally? You have not understood the power of service.

If you are not serving, you are a liability. Service opens doors, attracts favours, provides inner satisfaction, and sustains status. Service has a high reward. Service pays both now and in the future! Examples of service: *"for David, after he had served his own generation by the will of God, fell on sleep, and was laid unto his fathers, and saw decay."* Acts 13:36 Israel cannot forget David because he was a servant leader. Are you a servant leader? The people of Joppa cannot forget Dorcas' service because she was a community leader. The generation of Egyptians and Pharaohs cannot forget Joseph because he was a professional service leader. The likes of Kwame Nkrumah, Mahatma Ghandi, Abraham Lincoln, Dr. Martin Luther King Jr, Winston Churchill, and Nelson Mandela served their generations. Are you serving your generation? Who are you serving?

There is something in the corporate world called the Long Service Award. It started with Rebecca - she was patient enough to give water to ten thirsty camels! As a reward, Rebecca became the powerful wife of Isaac and the daughter in-law of wealthy Abraham - the friend of God, patriarch of three world famous religions, and father of faith.

Discover your talent and use it to serve your generation. The power of service will open doors for you this week. Shalom!

Prayer: Oh God give me the power to serve dilligently. Help me oh Lord to to choose service over mediocrity.

Quotation: *The best way to find yourself is to lose yourself in the service of others*. **-Mahatma Gandhi**

54

Where Is Your Ark?

"And the ark of God was taken; and the two sons of Eli, Hophni and Phinehas, were slain." 1 Sam 4:11

In the Old Testament, before the building of tabernacles and temples, the presence of God was symbolized by his Ark. The Ark of God contains three simple but significant things: a pot of manna, the rod of Aaron and the two stone tablets on which the Ten Commandments were written

To me, the three symbols signify unique things:

1. The manna simply tells you that God can provide the basic necessities of life, which are food, clothing and shelter. He demonstrated this to The Israelites when He carried them on eagles' wings. Ex 19:4
2. The Rod symbolizes what God has deposited in you. Call it the talent, anointing, charisma, beauty, treasures that make you who you are.
3. The tablet of the commandment represents God's final and ultimate decision. His judgment on how you have used his provisions of the two above.

So, we read about Eli, Hophni and Phinchas. The father, Eli, was accused by God of refusal to warn his children against a life that was ungodly. Put another way, that is of poor parenting or not taking care of his children. The two children were accused of failure to respect and have regard for the things of God. After God warned Eli and the children and they did not change, they both children died one day in a battle. You will be far from tragedy in Jesus name. It was really a striking blow as the Ark of God was also taken. The news of the capturing of the Ark of God and the death of his children prompted Eli to have a heart attack. He broke his neck and died.

You can give your interpretations to the symbols in the Ark of God, one thing you cannot deny is that The Ark represents the presence of God, therefore:

- ♦ Take care of the Ark of God.
- ♦ Don't be careless with the Ark of God.
- ♦ Don't devalue the Ark of God.
- ♦ Guard jealously the Ark of God.
- ♦ Preserve the Ark of God.

Failure to take care of the Ark of God (God's presence, represented by the Holy Ghost) has dangerous consequences. It leads to physical death, financial death, spiritual death and hell fire. My counsel for you this morning is not to repeat the mistakes of Eli, Hophni and Phinehas who took the things of God for granted and allowed the Ark of God to be taken away from them. My prayer for you and myself is that we shall not do anything that will make the Ark of God to be taken away from us in Jesus name. Pray for your Eli or your Hophni and Phinehas now! Jesus is Lord!

Prayer: Oh Lord let your mercy prevail. No matter the misbehaviour of my children don't kill them Oh God.

Quotation: *Death is not the greatest loss in life. The greatest loss is what dies inside us while we live.* **-Norman Cousins**

55

The Ark Of God Shall Not Fail You!

"And when they of Ashdod arose early on the morrow, behold, Dagon was fallen upon his face to the earth before the ark of the LORD. And they took Dagon, and set him in his place again.4.And when they arose early on the morrow morning, behold, Dagon was fallen upon his face to the ground before the ark of the LORD; and the head of Dagon and both the palms of his hands were cut off upon the threshold; only the stump of Dagon was left to him." 1 Sam 5: 3 & 4

When Israel was fighting the Philistines, they had a bad relationship with God and ignored that. They brought the Ark of God to the battled field and God allowed them to be defeated. 30, 000 of them were killed, Eli's sons died, even the Ark of God was captured! In that sense the Ark of God failed them.

The Philistines took that experience to mean that the Ark of God was powerless afterall - meaning the God of Israel was powerless. Really?

The Yorubas have a saying: *"aseyi to wu bi Eledumare,"* which means "God in His sovereignty does whatever pleases Him." Is that not also what Psalm 115:3 says? *"God is in heaven and does whatever please him."* I agree.

In the Scripture above, (I encourage you to read the entire chapter of 1 Samuel 5, very interesting and it shows the way God deals with powerless gods and their blind followers) it seems the Ark of God just 'woke up' to its responsibilities' and began to show the power that God was made of. It began to deal with the gods of the Philistines -or as the Americans will say, it began to hit the Philistines below the belt- where it matters. It was like a joke to them, the 'the ordinary box' that the Israelites were carrying could be kept anywhere, so they thought. They put it on Dagon's shrine.

By the time they woke up. Dagon had fallen flat. All the enemies of your life shall fall today in the name of Jesus!

The Philistines did not suspect anything, so thinking Dagon's fall was just a coincidence, they put him back in his spot- as if to say 'be a good boy, if this box they call the ark of God decides to fight you, give him the fight of his life. Just like the coaches tell their boxers in their different corners between the rounds. 'Throw your punches heavily', 'fight him with all your strength, 'show that you are a god too,' they say. But alas by the morning Dagon had been given a total knock out - when they looked they found him dismembered! "By the time you wake up tomorrow morning all the powers parading themselves as god shall be put to shame in the name of Jesus."

> "By the time you wake up tomorrow morning all the powers parading themselves as god shall be put to shame in the name of Jesus."

They hurriedly but shamefully carried the Ark of God out and according to the scriptures it brought them nothing but probems.

"But after they had moved it, the Lord's hand was against that city, throwing it into a great panic. He afflicted the people of the city, both young and old, with an outbreak of tumors." 1 Sam 5:9. All those who are reading this, my God will deal with all the Dagons against you in Jesus name.

So what is The Holy Spirit teaching us this morning?

1. There is no God like our God- He is not just the True God he is the living God.
2. Before our God all other gods must bow.
3. You cannot mock our God. At the mention of the name of Jesus every knee shall bow.
4. Our God cannot only fight for Himself he can fight for you and I.
5. Our enemies are too small for our God.
6. Even when we are sleeping our God who does not sleep or slumber is fighting on our behalf.
7. Our God has capacity to afflict our enemies with diseases.

Let me summarize by saying the Ark of God, the presence of God, shall not fail you!

Prayer: Oh Lord, let the Ark of God not fail me in Jesus name. Let every Dagon parading themselves in my life fall down shamefully in Jesus name.

Quotation: *So they set out from the mount of the Lord three days' journey. And the ark of the covenant of the Lord went before them three days' journey, to seek out a resting place for them* – Moses (Numbers 10:33)

56

Seven Ways To Secure The Gate Of Your Flourishing

"Lift up your heads, O ye gates; and be ye lift up, ye everlasting doors; and the King of glory shall come in." Psalm 24:7

There are some things that you must know about flourishing. There is a place where your allocation is in life is, the place where you are to flourish. There is need to locate that place. *"Now the Lord had said unto Abram, Get thee out of thy country, and from thy kindred, and from thy father's house, unto a land that I will shew thee."* Gen 12:1There is also a gate and a key securing it for you. You will need the right key to open the gate *"Enter into his gates with thanksgiving, and into his courts with praise: be thankful unto him, and bless his name. Psalm 100:4*

Below I have detailed the keys:

1. **The master key is the Bible**, read it! *"This book of the law shall not depart out of thy mouth; but thou shalt meditate therein day and night, that thou mayest observe to do according to all that is written therein: for then thou shalt make thy way prosperous, and then thou shalt have good success." Jos 1:8*

2. **Offer praises to God**. *"Then was our mouth filled with laughter, and our tongue with singing: then said they among the heathen, The Lord hath done great things for them" Psalm126:2*

3. **Pray at every stage on your journey to flourishing**, e.g. Lord help me to focus, help me not to be distracted, etc. *"Ask, and it shall be given you; seek, and ye shall find; knock, and it shall be opened unto you." Matt 7:7*

4. **Ensure you possess the right skills** (and if you already possess them, put them to use!). *"Now send me a skilled man to work in gold, silver, brass and iron, and in purple, crimson and violet fabrics, and who knows how to make engravings, to work with the skilled*

men whom I have in Judah and Jerusalem, whom David my father provided. 2 Chr 2:7. Flourishing is about meeting the needs of the other man who has your money in his pocket!

5. **Get the right team**. For instance if you are starting a company, a church, or any organization you cannot do it alone. Get the right person you can brainstorm, pray, and strategize with. The person could be your spouse, friend, sibling, or associate. You need a team. *"Two are better than one; because they have a good reward for their labour. 10 For if they fall, the one will lift up his fellow: but woe to him that is alone when he falleth; for he hath not another to help him up"* Ecc 4:9-10

6. **Hard work**. God put Adam in the garden to till the ground. You have to till the ground- whether you can afford to work smart using tractors or have nothing but hoes, cutlasses and your bare hands. It is up to you, you can not flourish without hard work. Hard work is the extra thing you do after your routine work. *"In the morning sow thy seed, and in the evening withhold not thine hand: for thou knowest not whether shall prosper, either this or that, or whether they both shall be alike good"*. Eccl 11:6. Every day has 24 hours. These 24 hours are broken down to three 8 hour segments. Each person has 8 hours to work and 8 hours to sleep. The extra 8 hours is to decide whether to be a billionaire or a beggar. It is a key to accessing flourishing. May you work hard.

7. **Persistence, persistence, persistence**! It takes time to flourish in your field of expertise. The amount of time varies from one individual to another because in your allocated place the water bed may be different. When you dig the earth you will reach water for your borehole. The water bed in Warri Delta State is shallow. The water bed in Igede-Ekiti, Ekiti State is deep. *"And let us not be weary in well doing: for in due season we shall reap, if we faint not."* Gal 9:6

Prayer Points

- If Canada is your place of allocation you will speak to Canada, Canada hear the word of God come forth with my flourishing. If where you are is not the place to flourish ask God to direct you to that place in this year of flourishing to the nation, state, city. Until Abram was directed he wallowed in idolatry and poverty. Gen 12:1.

♦ Ask God to help you select your team.

♦ Pray to develop the aptitude to worship God, work hard and persevere.

♦ Pray as led until by the Holy Spirit until you possess your possession and flourishing parcel. Jesus is Lord.

Prayer: O Lord, I now know that my allocation is my location, help me to locate my place of allocation and reach there by your grace.

Quotation: *You can talk all you want about having a clear purpose and strategy for your life, but ultimately this means nothing if you are not investing the resources you have in a way that is consistent with your strategy. In the end, a strategy is nothing but good intentions unless it's effectively implemented."* — **Clayton M. Christensen**

57

Endeavour To Finish Your Life Assignment.

"Then Moses raised his arm and struck the rock twice with his staff. Water gushed out, and the community and their livestock drank. But the LORD said to Moses and Aaron, because you did not trust in me enough to honor me as holy in the sight of the Israelites, you will not bring this community into the land I give them." Numbers 20:11-12

So many ministers and people generally do not finish their ministry or life assignment at all, not to talk of finishing well. That will not be our portion in Jesus name. Let me give some examples:

Moses did not take the Israelites to the land of Canaan because of anger, lack of trust in God, disobedience, and taking credit for God's work. "Must we [referring to Moses and Aaron] bring you water out of this rock?" (Num 20:10) even though he was the meekest man. His assignment was to take the people to the land and divide it for them. He did not, it took Joshua to finish it.

Elijah did not finish his assignment due to fear, even though he was one of the boldest prophets in the Bible and did great exploits by dealing with the prophets of Baal and Asteroth. Jezebel was provoked because of Elijah's exploits and how he dealt with her fake prophets so he ran in 1 King 19. It took Jehu and Elisha to finish it as we can see in 2 Kings 9-10.

Samson did not finish his assignment of delivering Israel from the Philistines and neighbouring enemies as God ordained for him before he was born in Judges 13:6. His ministry suffered due to carelessness, immorality and a lack of focus. Others in the failure category are many, your name will not appear there.

Saul, the King, did not finish his life assignment. He was engrossed in envy, unforgiveness, and bitterness against David. *"Then said Saul unto his armourbearer, Draw thy sword, and thrust me through therewith;*

lest these uncircumcised come and thrust me through, and abuse me. But his armourbearer would not; for he was sore afraid. Therefore Saul took a sword, and fell upon it." 1 King 31:4.

Demas was in the category of disciples and followers of Paul and he had a glorious future. His colleagues were Luke and John Mark who wrote the synoptic gospels with Matthew and John. But he left that and wandered into oblivion for he did not finish his life assignment. *For Demas hath forsaken me, having loved this present world, and is departed unto Thessalonica; Crescens to Galatia, Titus unto Dalmatia. 2 Tim 4:10*

On the other hand the Word also give us multiple examples of those who did finish their assignment well. Here are some examples:

Paul finished his assignment. In Act 9:15-16 God said he should take the gospel to the Gentiles and that was why he did not become an administrative apostle in Israel, but rather took to the nations as a missionary. He did that three times and ended up dying in a foreign land as a missionary in Rome. It was there he made that potent declaration:

"I have fought a good fight, I have finished my course, I have kept the faith: 8 Henceforth there is laid up for me a crown of righteousness, which the Lord, the righteous judge, shall give me at that day: and not to me only, but unto all them also that love his appearing" 2 Tim 4:7-10.

Jesus Christ accomplished his glorious life purpose. Jesus Christ -God incarnate- came to this world and went through several ordeals including the crucifixion. Jesus finished his life assignment, saving man from their many sins:*"and she shall bring forth a son, and thou shalt call his name Jesus: for he shall save his people from their sins. Matt 1:21. "I have glorified thee on the earth: I have finished the work which thou gavest me to do" John 17:4.*

The process of finishing life assignments may be cumbersome but it is not only desirable but also profitbale and glorious. Let us do our best and work extra hard, put our faith in Jesus Christ and endeavour to finish our life assignment.

Prayer. Oh Lord, help me finish my life assignment.

Quotation: *Ability is what you're capable of doing. Motivation determines what you do. Attitude determines how well you do it.* **– Lou Holtz**

58

Repair The Fallen Altar

*"And Elijah said unto all the people, Come near unto me.
And all the people came near unto him. And he repaired the
altar of the LORD that was broken down. And Elijah took
twelve stones, according to the number of the tribes of the sons
of Jacob, unto whom the word of the LORD came, saying,
Israel shall be thy name:"* 1 King 18:30-31

The theme of International Gatherings of Eagles (IGOE) Conference
in the year 2017 was 'Repair The Fallen Altars.' As the IGOE team and I
travelled around the world that year, specifically to, Liverpool, England;
Dublin, Ireland; Ostersund, Sweden; Chennai, India; Kathmandu, Nepal;
Lahore, Pakistan; Freetown, Sierra Leone; Monrovia, Liberia; Abidjan,
Cote D'ivoire; Accra, Ghana; and Lagos, Nigeria. I shared that there are
seven levels of altar to be repaired: personal, family, church, city, regional,
national, and continental altars.

Below are the altars that we need to fix in our lives, which will lead to
fixing the churches and if the churches are fixed the nations will be fixed.

1. The altar of truth
2. The altar of honesty
3. The altar of integrity
4. The altar of righteousness
5. The altar of unity
6. The altar of wisdom for governance
7. The altar of knowledge
8. The altar of no more corruption
9. The altar of serving the true God
10. The altar of praying the right prayer
11. The altar of nation building

12. The altar of accountability, transparency, hard work, entrepreneurship, trustworthiness, patriotism, sincerity, purity, care for this generation and the next generation and many more...

I have limited this to the biblical 12 stones that Elijah requested. We can rephrase, reshuffle, repackage these broad lines. We can even stretch to so many more across the nations, but these are the lines of altar that we need to repair, rebuild, raise, in prayer, attitude, character in the church and in the market place. Talk is cheap.

The solution is to start the repair. Elijah repaired. You are the Elijah of this generation. Let the repair of the altar start with you today. The issue of corruption in our lives, churches and nations is not unsolvable. It is a collective responsibility, that needs individual attention. If each of us can determine to follow the procedures for repair itemised, above we would have succeeded in our mission in fixing our churches nations.

Prayer: O Lord help me to repair my fallen altar. Help our churches and nations also to repair the altars.

Quotation: *And Elijah said unto all the people, Come near unto me. And all the people came near unto him. And he repaired the altar of the Lord that was broken down* - **Elijah the Tishbite (1 King 18:30)**

59

How To Avoid Reproach

"And they said unto me, The remnant that are left of the captivity there in the province are in great affliction and reproach...."

"Then said I unto them, Ye see the distress that we are in, how Jerusalem lieth waste, and the gates thereof are burned with fire: come, and let us build up the wall of Jerusalem, that we be no more a reproach." Neh 1:3; 2: 17.

Reproach is not desirable. Many things are responsible for reproach. It coud be traced to someone's background, for example a family known for mental health issues. It could be circumstantial, the type Naomi experienced when she left Israel for Moab and she lost husband and two sons. She desired they should change her name from Naomi (Sweetness) to Maara (bitterness) because of reproach. But the most terrible is doing things yourself that bring reproach. Watch your behaviour in the society. Nehemiah said paraphrased "we cannot afford to be in affliction and reproach. Let us do something about it, let us 'build our broken wall and broken life style." How do we avoid reproach?

Live a dignified life. Live a holy life. Live a sinless life. Live a joyful life. Live a life of integrity. Live a generous life. Live a respectable life. Live a dependable life.

Don't be a bully, don't be a whore, don't dress shabbily or immodestly, don't steal, don't be a 419ner (fraudse, don't be a wine bibber. Be drunk with Holy Spirit not with alcohol. Don't abuse your body with cocaine, heroin. marijuana, or cigarettes.

Carry yourself with respect and dignity, not only in church, but also in your office, your neighbourhood even your house.

Don't talk anyhow. Don't be a gossiper, an idolator, a party goer or murmurer. Don't be among the corrupters, abusers and spoilers. Don't be insolent and indolent. Don't embezzle public funds whether in government, school, industry or even church.

Love and pray for those involved in LGBT but avoid it as a plague because God detests it and destroyed Sodom and Gomorrah because of it. Youth, don't be involved in gangs and guns, but rather be prayerful and mighty in scriptures. Don't be involved in assassinations, killings, raping, incest, kidnapping, or armed robbery. You are a new man/woman as in 2 Corinthians 5:16. Walk in the spirit and not in the flesh as stated in Galatians 5:16-21. As a man, provide for and protect your family. Love your wife. As a woman, respect and submit to your husband. Stop nagging! Have a great life by avoiding a life style that will bring reproach to you and your family.

Be an eagle believer not a chicken. After preaching on this recently in Lahore, Pakistan, my interpreter helped me put it this way. "You can eat chicken but don't be a chicken!" I totally agree.

Prayer: Lord help me to stop everything I am doing that is bringing reproach to my life. Help me to avoid reproach.

Quotation: *I think it better to do right, even if we suffer in so doing, than to incur the reproach of our consciences and posterity.* - **Robert E. Lee**

60

Thirty Tips On How To Make Your Marriage Work.

"Set me as a seal upon your heart, as a seal upon your arm, for love is strong as death, jealousy is fierce as the grave. Its flashes are flashes of fire, the very flame of the LORD. Many waters cannot quench love, neither can floods drown it. If a man offered for love all the wealth of his house, he would be utterly despised." - Solomon 8:6

1. Stop finding the faults of your spouse.
2. Start finding reasons to celebrate your spouse.
3. Stop finding reasons why the marriage cannot work.
4. Start finding reasons why the marriage must work.
5. Stop documenting facts to nail your spouse.
6. Start documenting milestones in your spouse's achievements.
7. Stop making unreasonable demands of your spouse.
8. Start evaluating his/her limitations and do your best to remove them where you can
9. Stop calling your spouse negative names or using derogatory terminologies even when it is true, e.g. liar, selfish, dumb, etc. etc. Words are like eggs, once they fall on the ground and shatter you can never recover them.
10. Start using words that will build your spouse up, even in moments of anger. Remember the dust always settles but memories linger.
11. Stop cursing your spouse because curses destroy. You will both carry the effect of the curses with your generations to come.
12. Start blessing your spouse. You both will enjoy the effect of the blessing as well as your coming generations.
13. Stop finding reasons why you cannot pray together.
14. Start finding reasons why you can pray together and please pray together.

15. Stop finding reasons you cannot have sex together.
16. Start finding reasons to have sex together. Sex is not just a tonic and a stimulant, it is a mystery that creates not just therapies for bonding but platforms for new beginnings. God the designer new why He created sexual components in marriage.
17. Stop using sex as toll gates.
18. Start using sex as blessing gates.
19. Stop blaming your spouse for your marital woes.
20. Start blaming yourself for your marital instability. In that sense you too should look for solutions.
21. Stop ignoring simple words that can help your marriage.
22. Start applying words that can heal your marital wounds.
23. Stop doing things that will deliberately hurt your spouse.
24. Start doing what will make your spouse fulfill his or her destiny.
25. Stop planning for divorce.
26. Start planning for enjoyable and lasting marriage.
27. Wives, stop disrespecting your husband. It is God's command and it will help your marriage beyond your expectations
28. Husbands, start loving your wife. Your wife genuinely needs love. It is God's command.
29. Husbands, stop finding reasons not to provide for your household. Be responsible.
30. Wives, start finding ways to support the family finances, your husband may not be able to shoulder all the responsibility.

Prayer: Pray that in all circumstances you will keep making your marriage work and that God will help you make your marriage work.

Quotation : "Success in marriage does not come merely through finding the right mate, but through being the right mate." ~ Barnett Brickner

OTHER BOOKS BY PASTOR AMOS DELE DADA

ORDER ONLINE TODAY FROM AMAZON, EBAY,
CACBETHEL.COM OR IGOEMINISTRY.COM

CONTACT AUTHOR DIRECTLY AT
AMOS.DADA@GMAIL.COM

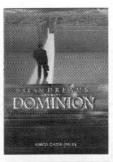

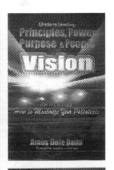

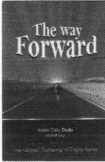

Printed in the United States
By Bookmasters